SITTING BULL

SITTING BULL

A Biography

Edward J. Rielly

GREENWOOD BIOGRAPHIES

GREENWOOD PRESS
WESTPORT, CONNECTICUT • LONDON

Library of Congress Cataloging-in-Publication Data

Rielly, Edward J.
  Sitting Bull : a biography / Edward J. Rielly.
    p. cm. — (Greenwood biographies, ISSN 1540–4900)
  Includes bibliographical references and index.
  ISBN-13: 978–0–313–33809–0 (alk. paper)
  ISBN-10: 0–313–33809–4 (alk. paper)
 1. Sitting Bull, 1834?–1890. 2. Dakota Indians—Kings and rulers—Biography.
3. Dakota Indians—Wars. 4. Dakota Indians—Government relations. I. Title.
  E99.D1.S615 2007
  978.004'9752440092—dc22
  [B]
                                              2007016139

British Library Cataloguing in Publication Data is available.

Library of Congress Catalog Card Number: 2007016139
ISBN-13: 978–0–313–33809–0
ISBN-10: 0–313–33809–4
ISSN: 1540–4900

First published in 2007

Greenwood Press, 88 Post Road West, Westport, CT 06881
An imprint of Greenwood Publishing Group, Inc.
www.greenwood.com

Printed in the United States of America

The paper used in this book complies with the
Permanent Paper Standard issued by the National
Information Standards Organization (Z39.48–1984).

10 9 8 7 6 5 4 3 2 1

CONTENTS

Photo essay follows page 74.

SERIES FOREWORD

In response to high school and public library needs, Greenwood developed this distinguished series of full-length biographies specifically for student use. Prepared by field experts and professionals, these engaging biographies are tailored for high school students who need challenging yet accessible biographies. Ideal for secondary school assignments, the length, format, and subject areas are designed to meet educators' requirements and students' interests.

Greenwood offers an extensive selection of biographies spanning all curriculum-related subject areas including social studies, the sciences, literature and the arts, history and politics, as well as popular culture, covering public figures and famous personalities from all time periods and backgrounds, both historical and contemporary, who have made an impact on American and/or world culture. Greenwood biographies were chosen based on comprehensive feedback from librarians and educators. Consideration was given to both curriculum relevance and inherent interest. The result is an intriguing mix of the well known and the unexpected, the saints and sinners from long-ago history and contemporary pop culture. Readers will find a wide array of subject choices from fascinating crime figures like Al Capone to inspiring pioneers like Margaret Mead, from the greatest minds of our time like Stephen Hawking to the most amazing success stories of our day like J. K. Rowling.

Although the emphasis is on fact, not glorification, the books are meant to be fun to read. Each volume provides in-depth information about the subject's life from birth through childhood, the teen years, and adulthood. A thorough account relates family background and education, traces personal and professional influences, and explores struggles, accomplishments, and contributions. A timeline highlights the most significant life events against a historical perspective. Bibliographies supplement the reference value of each volume.

ACKNOWLEDGMENTS

I am deeply appreciative of the support I have received from Saint Joseph's College, including a faculty fellowship to help with expenses involved in writing this biography. My research has been facilitated by the generous assistance of the staffs of the Saint Joseph's College Library, the University of Maine library system, and the McCracken Research Library of the Buffalo Bill Historical Center in Cody, Wyoming. As always, the support of my wife, Jeanne, has been immeasurable.

INTRODUCTION

Sitting Bull was the greatest American Indian leader of his time, perhaps the greatest American leader of the nineteenth century with the probable exception of Abraham Lincoln. His virtues encompassed all of the most desirable characteristics of his Hunkpapa culture. He was enormously brave, demonstrating his courage in single combat, by risking his life to count coup (that is, touching an enemy), and in other ways, such as sitting down in full view (and shooting range) of American soldiers and calmly smoking his pipe, what his nephew White Bull called the bravest act he ever saw. Courage was a requisite for a leader, and it helped Sitting Bull earn his position as a war chief.

What set Sitting Bull apart from other leaders, though, was not just his courage or skill in battle against Indian enemies such as the Crows or U.S. troops but the wide range of his attributes. He was a true spiritual leader who felt very much in touch with Wakantanka and by all accounts sincerely believed that he had received visions and dreams in which the spirit world communicated with him. Closely attuned to the world around him, he also believed himself able to understand the communications of animals and birds.

The most significant of Sitting Bull's visions occurred shortly before the Battle of Little Bighorn. After participating in the Sun Dance, he received a vision of soldiers falling from the sky upside down, which he interpreted to mean a great victory for his people in the upcoming battle. That vision inspired and emboldened the Lakotas, helping to ensure a decisive victory over George Armstrong Custer and his Seventh Cavalry in one of the most famous battles in American history.

That battle earned Sitting Bull lasting fame, or infamy, putting him at the top of the list of Indians that the U.S. government most wanted to capture. Yet to remember him solely because of his victory over Custer does a great injustice to this multifaceted leader.

Sitting Bull was deeply revered by his own people for what today might be called his "family values." As was common in the Lakota culture, he took multiple wives, but even that demonstrated his generosity and compassion. When he sought to make Four Robes his wife, for example, he also accepted her older sister, Seen by the Nation, despite her having two sons, one a deaf-mute. Sitting Bull even gave up his treasured horse Bloated Jaw for her. He loved his many children dearly and suffered great sorrow when one of his children died. He was close to his parents and, after his father's death, took in his mother, Her Holy Door, who lived with him for the rest of her life. Sitting Bull's uncle, Four Horns, was a staunch friend and supporter of his nephew until his death about three years before Sitting Bull's own death. Sitting Bull also had a close relationship with his nephews, One Bull and White Bull, who, long after their uncle's death, when they themselves were old men, passed along many stories of Sitting Bull's greatness to Sitting Bull's first great biographer, Stanley Vestal.

Along with the victory over Custer, casual readers of history are likely to know one additional fact about Sitting Bull: that he joined Buffalo Bill Cody's Wild West Show. Sitting Bull did indeed join Cody in the summer of 1885 for about four months. Cody treated him with great respect, refusing to sensationalize his star performer as the killer of Custer, as newspapers often portrayed him. As Sitting Bull left Cody to return to Standing Rock Reservation, the famous showman and former buffalo hunter and army scout gave him the trick-performing horse that Sitting Bull had ridden in the show. Then Sitting Bull went home.

Home for Sitting Bull, though, was not truly the reservation but the Plains, where he and his Hunkpapas could move freely to follow the buffalo that supplied the necessities of life and live out the traditions of their ancestors. Sitting Bull became, for many native peoples, an abiding symbol of resistance to efforts by the U.S. government to take their land, their freedom, and their way of life. That perception of Sitting Bull made the triumph at Little Bighorn possible.

The victory at Little Bighorn showed Sitting Bull at the apex of his power and influence. Thousands of Indians, principally Lakotas and Cheyennes, congregated around him because they understood clearly his strength and determination to remain faithful to their cherished traditions. He was a magnet, attracting those who wished to continue living as their ancestors had lived. No one else could have gathered the vast numbers who were drawn to him in the summer of 1876 and inspired them as did Sitting Bull. Without Sitting Bull there would have been no victory at Little Bighorn, and probably not even a battle.

Yet that victory, the greatest ever by American Indians over the U.S. military, also planted the seeds of Sitting Bull's defeat. The U.S. government and large numbers of U.S. citizens, who quickly began to mythologize Custer, demanded retribution, and great resources were put into defeating Sitting Bull. Forced into exile in Canada, Sitting Bull bided his time, hoping that somehow he could maintain a past that was rapidly dissolving. Finally, the buffalo disappeared and his people were without food. To save his followers from starvation, he led them back to the United States and surrendered at Fort Buford, knowing that his own life would be drastically changed. The ultimate tragedy, which Sitting Bull certainly understood, was that the whole Lakota way of life would likely come to an end. And it did, but Sitting Bull continued to struggle against that end as long as he lived.

Sitting Bull spent the final portion of his life, almost a decade, living a reservation existence he had fought so hard against. Even during those final years, Sitting Bull did what he could to maintain some connection to his cultural past and give his people hope. When the Ghost Dance arrived in the Dakotas, Sitting Bull supported it, surely not because he believed it would completely restore the world of his youth, but because he saw in the ritual a vehicle within which to maintain some portion of the Lakota way. He may have been grasping at straws with the Ghost Dance, but Sitting Bull was not about giving up hope.

And Sitting Bull did not give up until two fellow Lakotas, tribal policemen named Bull Head and Red Tomahawk, shot and killed him while attempting to arrest him. The arrest was ordered by representatives of the government that had tried for so many years to defeat Sitting Bull and, after his surrender, to transform him into an imitation white man. Sitting Bull did not die an imitation of anything. He was an original, a unique individual who excelled in all aspects of his Hunkpapa culture. Sitting Bull deserves to be remembered not primarily as the slayer of Custer but as one of the greatest individuals that the land now known as the United States has ever produced.

This biography examines Sitting Bull's life in a generally chronological manner and within the cultural context of Lakota culture as it existed in the second half of the nineteenth century. It is not possible to adequately understand Sitting Bull without understanding the values that shaped him and by which he tried to live.

Also included in this biography are learning aids. One is the timeline that offers many of the major events in Sitting Bull's life. The timeline notes important actions that Sitting Bull took as well as historical events that in significant ways affected him and his way of life.

A bibliography consisting of print and electronic sources follows the chapters. The bibliography both documents the research that went into this book and provides additional reading and research options for those who would like to learn more about Sitting Bull. Books are emphasized over journal and magazine articles because they are easier for most students, especially in high schools, to locate. Regarding the electronic sources, readers are cautioned that Web addresses often change.

The photographs chosen for the book reflect a number of incidents and people important in Sitting Bull's life as well as images of Sitting Bull himself. No photographs of the young Sitting Bull exist, but two pictographic images drawn by Sitting Bull himself offer depictions of his actions before the earliest existing photographs of him.

TIMELINE: EVENTS IN THE LIFE OF SITTING BULL

1831   Sitting Bull, originally named Jumping Badger, is probably born in this year along the Grand River in present-day South Dakota.

1846   Jumping Badger counts his first coup and is honored by his father with the new name Sitting Bull.

1847   Probably in this year, Sitting Bull suffers his first wound in a fight with the Flatheads.

1851   The Fort Laramie Treaty authorizes construction of forts and roads and establishes boundaries for individual tribes, but no Hunkpapas sign it.

1856   A wound inflicted by a Crow leaves Sitting Bull with a permanent limp.

1857   Sitting Bull spares the life of a Hohe youth. He also becomes a war chief.

1859   Jumping Bull, Sitting Bull's father, is killed in a battle with Crows. Sitting Bull gives his father's name to the Hohe youth whom he has adopted as a brother.

1862   The U.S. government authorizes construction of a transcontinental railroad and enacts the Homestead Act to open up settlements in the West. Members of the Dakota division of the Sioux turn to armed rebellion in Minnesota.

1863   The Battles of Dead Buffalo Lake and Stony Lake mark the beginning of open warfare between Sitting Bull's Hunkpapas and the U.S. military.

1864   At Killdeer Mountain on July 28, Sitting Bull engages in his first major battle with the U.S. military. In September, Sitting Bull is shot in the left hip during another encounter with U.S. soldiers.

1865   The Sioux and U.S. government sign nine treaties, although Sitting Bull is not involved.

1868   Father De Smet visits Sitting Bull on a peace mission. The Treaty of 1868 sets up the Great Sioux Reservation while the army agrees to abandon the Bozeman Trail forts, but Sitting Bull does not participate in the negotiations and does not sign the treaty.

1869   Four Horns leads a successful effort to have Sitting Bull, his nephew, made supreme leader of the Lakotas. Sitting Bull leads his Hunkpapas to a victory known as the Thirty Crows Killed Battle.

1870   Sitting Bull is wounded in the arm during a battle against the Flatheads.

1872   Sitting Bull marries the sisters Four Robes and Seen by the Nation. During a summer engagement against U.S. troops, Sitting Bull calmly smokes his pipe within firing range of the soldiers.

1874   Custer leads an expedition to search for gold in the Black Hills.

1875   Sitting Bull organizes and dances in a large Sun Dance to help unify the Lakotas. The U.S. government fails in its attempt to buy the Black Hills.

1876   All Sioux are ordered to report to reservations by January 31 or be considered hostile. After the Battles of Powder River and the Rosebud and Sitting Bull's vision of U.S. soldiers falling upside down into his camp, a massive force primarily consisting of Lakota bands defeats Custer and the Seventh Cavalry at the Little Bighorn in June. Custer and everyone with him are killed.

1877   Sitting Bull, pursued by Colonel Bear Coat Miles, enters Canada in May. Crazy Horse surrenders during the same month and is killed in September.

1881   Sitting Bull arrives at Fort Buford on July 19 to surrender. He is transferred to Fort Yates, arriving on August 1, and is moved to Fort Randall in September.

1883   Sitting Bull returns to Standing Rock Agency on May 10.

1884   Sitting Bull joins an exhibition tour entitled the "Sitting Bull
       Combination," organized by Alvaren Allen, in September.
1885   William F. "Buffalo Bill" Cody hires Sitting Bull for his Wild
       West Show. Sitting Bull performs with Cody during the
       summer and becomes friends with Annie Oakley.
1888   Sitting Bull strongly resists the Sioux Act of 1888. He travels
       to Washington, D.C., with a contingent of chiefs and meets
       President Benjamin Harrison.
1889   The Lakotas agree to individual allotments of land and
       division of the Great Sioux Reservation into six smaller
       reservations.
1890   The Ghost Dance begins among the Lakotas. Sitting Bull be-
       comes friends with Mary Collins and Catherine Weldon. He is
       killed by tribal policemen on December 15 when they attempt
       to arrest him. The burial occurs at the Fort Yates military
       cemetery on December 17. The massacre of Big Foot and his
       people on December 29 ends any substantial opposition by the
       Sioux.
1953   Sitting Bull's remains are moved to a location near Mobridge,
       South Dakota.

Chapter 1

BORN TO THE SIOUX NATION
(1831–1845)

BIRTH OF JUMPING BADGER

Neither the location nor precise date of the birth of Sitting Bull, perhaps the greatest of all American Indian leaders, is known with certainty. Sitting Bull's two most prominent biographers, Stanley Vestal and Robert Utley, conclude that he most likely was born at Many Caches, named for storage pits on the south bank of the Grand River, near present-day Bullhead, South Dakota. They also opt for 1831 as the probable year of his birth, a time when the Lakota Sioux were approaching their peak as the most dominant people of the Great Plains. Vestal conducted extensive interviews during the 1920s and 1930s with elderly Lakotas, who as young men had known Sitting Bull. He suggests that Sitting Bull was born in the late winter of 1831, known as the Winter When Yellow Eyes Played in the Snow.[1]

The Lakotas gave names rather than numbers to years. A prominent way to keep track of a tribe's history was the winter count, recorded in pictographs on a deer hide. Each year received a name based on a significant event from that year. An important member of the tribe painted the annual symbols representing the historical events in spiral form, starting at the vortex, or center, and spiraling outward in concentric circles. Months also were noted and named, for example, April as the Moon of the Birth of Calves.[2] Sitting Bull's original name was Jumping Badger. His father carried the name that he later would impart to his son—Tatanka-Iyotanka, or Sitting Bull. Sitting Bull's mother's name was Her Holy Door. An older sister, Good Feather, preceded Jumping Badger by six years. Another sister,

Brown Shawl Woman, also known as Twin Woman, would follow Jumping Badger. Fool Dog, the son of the elder Sitting Bull and an earlier wife, also was a member of the family. Before long, Jumping Badger inherited a nickname, Hunkesni, which means slow—not slow intellectually, but deliberate in his actions, a trait that in later years would manifest itself in the careful planning and wisdom that, along with his courage and spiritual nature, helped to make him deeply respected and honored.

HISTORY OF THE SIOUX

Hunkesni was born into a people whose identity had begun forming as early as the late thirteenth century when a number of tribal groups started establishing an alliance in what would become northwestern Wisconsin and central Minnesota. Later known by European descendants as the Sioux, they gradually began moving southward and westward as a result of what archaeologists refer to as "push" and "pull" forces.[3] The Sioux were pushed from the East by other tribes, including the Ojibwa, and by Euroamericans moving westward. At the same time, the promise of horses and a wide array of game to hunt, especially the buffalo, pulled them farther west.

The name *Sioux* came from the Ojibwa word *na-towe-ssiwa*, meaning aliens or enemies. The French converted the term to *Naudoweissious*, and English speakers shortened it to the easier to pronounce *Sioux*. The Sioux consisted of three main divisions. The easternmost Dakota (also called the Santee) consisted of four subdivisions that migrated into southern Minnesota along the Minnesota and Mississippi Rivers by the eighteenth century. The Yankton and Yanktonai (the two sometimes considered subgroups of one larger unit, the Nakota) crossed the Red River into southeastern South Dakota. The western division of the Sioux, the Lakota, also known as the Teton, consisted of seven subdivisions: Oglala, Brulé, Miniconjou, Two Kettle, Sans Arc, Hunkpapa, and Blackfeet (not to be confused with a separate Blackfeet tribe). The four Dakota subdivisions, the Yankton and Yanktonai, and the Lakota were considered the Oceti Sakowin, that is, the Seven Council Fires, composing the original ancestral units. Early references to the Sioux often are confusing, as many accounts incorrectly apply the name "Dakota" as a blanket term covering all Sioux.

Within each tribe, the basic social unit was the tiyospaye, or band, essentially an extended family. The tiyospaye changed as a result of births, deaths, marriages, and voluntary joining and leaving of the band. On occasion, an individual's serious misdeeds would lead to expulsion. A group of tiyospaye made up a subdivision of the Sioux, often called a tribe, such as the Hunkpapas.

The Lakota, the Council Fire into which Hunkesni was born, lived in the Northern Plains, with the Lakota territory stretching from the Missouri River in the East to the mouth of the Yellowstone River (Elk River to the Lakotas) in the West, from the Canadian border in the North to the Platte and Republican Rivers in the South. The Lakotas thus ranged over the present-day Dakotas as well as Wyoming, northern Nebraska, and southeastern Montana.

The elder Sitting Bull's tribe, the Hunkpapas, a name that means Campers at the Opening of the Circle,[4] lived between the Missouri and the Yellowstone Rivers. Although each Lakota tribe had its own territory, some of the smaller groups, such as the Hunkpapas, Sans Arcs, and Blackfeet, often camped together. Communication among the Sioux tribes was easy, as all spoke dialects of the same Siouan language and had no trouble understanding each other. Communicating with other tribes, however, often was extremely difficult, necessitating development of a common sign language.[5]

LAKOTA CULTURE

The Lakota culture was highly spiritual, and the future Sitting Bull would achieve as much renown for his visionary and spiritual gifts as for his skill in warfare. There was no separation of church and state among the Lakotas, as the divine permeated every aspect of the visible and invisible worlds.

Hunkesni would have learned early in his life about the deities that surrounded him. Sixteen deities inhabited various aspects of the world and exercised control over different dimensions of human life. Four of them were the most exalted: Wi, the sun, who was the chief of the gods; Skan, the sky, revered as the all-powerful spirit; Maka, the earth, viewed as the primal ancestor; and Inyan, the rock, the source and thus the foundation of all things. Together the gods constituted Wakantanka, the Great Mystery, and were individual manifestations of Wakantanka.[6]

The lowest order of deities, including the wanagi, resided within humans. When a person died the individual's wanagi needed to cross the river separating this life and the next one. If it failed to do so, it would wander forever in this world rather than pass into the spirit world. Each person also was believed to possess a niya, or ghost, and a sicun, or guardian. The niya entered at birth and imparted the ni, or life, to the person. The sicun acted like a conscience, aiding the individual to determine right from wrong; it also warned of danger, thus guarding both one's physical and moral well-being. A Christian might see striking similarities between the soul and the wanagi, the individual conscience and the sicun, and the concept of the Trinity and

Wakantanka, the latter consisting of 16 persons rather than 3, but all possessing the same essence and ultimately forming one rather than completely separate individuals.

The history of Hunkesni's people was part of the knowledge that he learned as a child, especially the story of White Buffalo Woman and her gift of the sacred Buffalo Calf Pipe to the Lakotas. According to Lakota belief, in the distant past two young men were camping when a beautiful woman appeared to them. One of the men saw her only as a desirable human and made sexual advances, whereupon a large cloud descended around him, leaving behind nothing but a few bones. The other young man correctly recognized her as wakan, that is, divine. She informed him that she was bringing the sacred Buffalo Calf Pipe to his people.

Rushing home, the young man told of the beautiful woman who was coming. She subsequently appeared, either completely naked or dressed in beautiful deerskin of many colors depending on the precise account. She served a great feast to all the Lakotas and then took the pipe from a pouch. She filled it with tobacco, smoked the pipe briefly, and then passed it to the chief. She assured the Lakotas that whenever they smoked the pipe, she would be present, hear their prayers, and intercede with Wakantanka on their behalf.

White Buffalo Woman gave them directions for preparing the tobacco and preserving the pipe. She also told them to perform seven rituals that would help maintain their welfare, including the individual vision quest, purification through a sweat bath, and the Sun Dance. When she departed in a cloud of smoke from a circle of burning sweetgrass, the Lakotas understood that the beautiful woman was White Buffalo Woman, also known as Wohpe, created by Skan, the sky god, to be the mediator between the human and spirit worlds.

Maintaining the pipe was a serious responsibility and being charged with that duty a great honor. Sitting Bull's nephew, White Bull, described how during 1897–98 the Indian agent at the Cheyenne River Agency confiscated the sacred pipe, apparently to force greater conformity to the Euroamerican culture. The assigned keeper, Elk Head, enlisted White Bull's help in restoring the pipe, which White Bull managed to do. Further testimony to the solemn obligation imposed by the pipe occurs in the book *Sitting Bull's Pipe*, by Kenneth B. Tankersley and Robert B. Pickering. They note that in the year 2005, Arvol Looking Horse was the 19th-generation member of his family to be charged with preserving the sacred pipe for the Lakotas.[7]

THE SUN DANCE

Among all of the religious ceremonies that Hunkesni witnessed and later participated in, the Sun Dance was the most significant. The Sun

Dance, in honor of Wi, the sun god, occurred annually, typically around June, and was designed to foster spiritual and social rebirth for the Lakotas. The buffalo god, Tatanka—god of ceremonies, health, and provision—also figured importantly in the ceremony, and after the dance the tribe would set out on its buffalo hunts.

The central portion of the Sun Dance (preparation of the Sun Dance Lodge and the dancing itself) took four days, with the actual dancing occurring on the third and fourth days, but was preceded by eight days of reflection, instruction, and preparation. The Sun Dance took place in a dance lodge constructed for that purpose. The lodge was enclosed within two circular fences of forked posts, with the center portion left open to the sky. Poles laid on the tops of the two rows of posts supported branches, creating a shaded resting place. The dancing area was in the open, middle portion of the lodge.

The Sun Dance Pole, made from a cottonwood tree, was the most important structural element in the Sun Dance Lodge. Complex rules governed the selection, cutting, and preparation of the tree. The pole was erected in the middle of the inner circle, surrounded by stakes driven into the ground. Male dancers were tied to the stakes, with the Sun Dance Pole reserved for an individual seeking to establish his special holiness and qualifications to be a shaman, or holy man, also known as a Wichasha Wakan. The dancers would be tethered to the pole or stakes in a manner that was extremely painful. Two sets of parallel slits would be cut in the person's chest, or sometimes in the back, and two wooden skewers inserted under the skin. A rope then was tied to each skewer and connected to the pole or a stake. Any slip could cause extraordinary anguish as the skin pulled or even ripped. Women and even children might also dance the Sun Dance but were not attached to the stakes.

The Sun Dance involved many rituals and symbols. It included specific methods of preparation for the dance, fasting requirements during the dancing, painting of bodies and clothing in colors such as red and blue that conveyed spiritual meanings (red symbolizing holiness, blue representing the heavens), and ritualistic use of a buffalo head and a sacred pipe. The Sun Dance was also a time to pierce the ears of Lakota children who had not yet taken that important step, the pierced ear signifying that the person would live according to Lakota customs.[8]

THE BUFFALO

With the Sun Dance concluded, the Lakotas would soon set off for their buffalo hunt. This was no sport; nor was it a casual hunt for a delicacy or just one source of food among many. It was a collective effort to acquire the very means whereby the Lakotas lived. The buffalo god appropriately represented provision for the Lakotas, as the animal supplied a vast array of life's necessities. The buffalo's sacred purpose was to ensure that the Lakotas would survive as a people. Since the appearance of the White Buffalo Woman, the Lakotas and the buffalo had been virtually one, with the buffalo giving life to the people as surely as individual men and women gave life to their children.

So much depended on the buffalo, including means of nourishment and protection from the elements. Individuals even looked to the buffalo for moral inspiration. The buffalo, for example, was honored as a strong, determined, courageous animal that would continue its forward course even in the face of a raging blizzard. It would never give up.[9]

The buffalo, also known as bison, was a huge animal. The male stood taller than most men—five and one-half to six and one-half feet at the shoulder, and it could reach over eleven feet in length. Despite its considerable weight—1,400 to 2,200 pounds—it could run as fast as many horses, reaching perhaps 35 miles per hour. A fast hunting horse could outrace buffalo over a short span, but the buffalo's endurance permitted it eventually to outdistance even the finest horses. The cows were smaller than the bulls, but they, as well as their calves, could maintain a high rate of speed.[10]

The Lakotas depended on the buffalo for food. Fresh meat was highly prized, and after a hunt, about one hundred Lakotas could consume two or three buffalo daily.[11] Buffalo meat also was prepared for winter use. Women would cut the buffalo meat into strips, dry it on racks, perhaps lightly smoke the strips, and store them in parfleches (sheets of rawhide folded around the contents and sewed up to form traveling cases). Such dried meet is often called "jerky." Another approach was to cook the meat, pound it into paste, pack it in rawhide bags or sections of the large intestine, pour in melted fat (sometimes adding berries, the ascorbic acid in berries helping to preserve the meat), and flatten the package for ease in transporting. The latter was known as pemmican and would keep almost indefinitely.[12] Buffalo meat today is recognized as a relatively healthy food, with more protein and less fat than beef.

The buffalo, though, served many more purposes than food. The skull was used in ceremonies, including the Sun Dance. Buffalo hides provided tipi covers, clothing, moccasins, blankets, shields, the tops of drums, gun cases, and many other items. Knives, arrowheads, war clubs, and paintbrushes were fashioned from buffalo bones. Cooking and storing utensils came from the animal's stomach and other internal organs. Buffalo chips (dried buffalo manure) served as fuel. Horns yielded cups, rattles, and ladles. Thread and bowstrings came from the buffalo's sinews. Even the blood proved useful for making paint.

The buffalo filled up much of Her Holy Door's day, as it did for other Lakota women.[13] In addition to preparing the meat for future consumption, women were responsible for tanning buffalo hides—an arduous process of drying, scraping, and softening—and then making the hides into clothing, tipi covers, and other objects. The Lakota woman's responsibility extended from making to maintaining. It was her role to take down the tipi with its buffalo hide cover, pack it and the family possessions, transport them to the next site, and put the tipi back up. On the journey from one site to the next, she would use a horse travois, a frame hung between two poles and dragged behind a horse, to move these possessions. When Sitting Bull was an infant, he rode on his mother's back in a cradleboard, which was a basket made from buffalo hide and attached to a board. A diaper of dried moss would help keep him clean, and a hole in the bottom of the cradleboard allowed the inevitable wetting to occur with a minimum of discomfort.

No one knows precisely how many buffalo roamed the western United States during Sitting Bull's youth, but firsthand accounts indicate huge numbers. Visitors noted herds that took an hour to pass at a gallop and extended several miles across. Estimates of the total buffalo population range up to 70 million. Tom McHugh in *The Time of the Buffalo* offers a carefully reasoned estimate of 34million. Whatever the total, the vast herds supplied the needs of the Lakotas and other tribes with plenty of buffalo left to replenish their numbers until the large-scale hunting by Euroamericans during the nineteenth century. Then, in a relatively short space of time, Euroamericans rendered the buffalo almost extinct as they killed buffalo for hides to make coats and other apparel, farmed buffalo bones for use in fertilizer, and executed a policy of buffalo extermination to reduce Indian tribes to dependency on the U.S. government (if not to exterminate the Indians as well). By the time of Sitting Bull's death in 1890, the total number of buffalo in the wild numbered about 300.[14]

NECESSARY SKILLS

Hunkesni learned to ride well at an early age, as did all Lakota boys. The horse stood beside the buffalo in importance. It was required for hunting, war, and normal travel. The migratory behavior of the buffalo, which needed to keep moving toward fresh grass, compelled the Lakotas to adopt the buffalo's mobile habits and made the horse essential.

Horses had once lived in North America but had died out during the last Ice Age. Spanish conquistadors reintroduced horses in the sixteenth century, and horses gradually spread from Mexico northward. As Hunkesni was growing up, his Hunkpapa Lakotas, like other tribes, had two main ways to acquire horses: by capturing wild horses or stealing them from other tribes. Possessing horses was essential not only to the buffalo hunt but also to maintaining the flexibility of movement that the Plains Indians needed to move from one campsite to another. Horses also were crucial in warfare, where they provided the means of attack as well as protection. A skilled horseman, as Hunkesni quickly became, could ride a horse with his body pressed to the horse's side, using the animal as a shield. With a heel over its back and an elbow in a loop of buffalo hair braided into the horse's mane, he could reach over the horse's back or stretch under its neck to shoot arrows. Because of its practical use, the horse became a primary measure of wealth as well as of generosity. Few gifts could match a horse in value.[15]

As a child, Hunkesni learned the skills that he would need in the two most crucial tasks of a man: hunting and fighting. Even the games he played developed these skills. Children were highly valued, and parents and grandparents showered affection on the Lakota children. They were the people's future, and they received steady instruction without physical punishment. Children were indulged in their desire to play, an indulgence owing much to the adults' understanding that play was a prelude to adult life. Hunkesni was fast in foot races, a skill directly related to success in war. A hoop game popular with the Hunkpapas, in which opposing teams used sticks to roll hoops into the other team's zone, encouraged competitiveness. Swimming bred endurance, horse races fostered necessary horsemanship, the Spear-and-Hoop-game required skill in handling a spear as the boys tried to throw spears through a hoop tossed into the air, and a variety of other games helped Hunkesni develop additional practical skills.[16]

HUNKESNI'S FIRST BUFFALO HUNT

An early milestone in Hunkesni's life occurred when, at 10 years of age, he participated in a buffalo hunt, putting to use some of the skills that he had been honing during childhood play. The Lakotas had two primary methods for hunting buffalo. One involved driving buffalo over a cliff. One individual, the Buffalo Caller, dressed in buffalo robes, enticed the herd toward the cliff. Men and women lined up along two sides, their lines gradually angling inward to form a V at the cliff's edge. As the buffalo approached the Buffalo Caller, the Lakotas along the two arms of the V shouted and waved buffalo robes to frighten the animals, forcing the stampeding herd toward the apex of the V. The Buffalo Caller obviously occupied a most dangerous position, and once the herd started stampeding, he had to move quickly to the side to prevent the onrushing animals from forcing him over the cliff. The rest of the Lakotas, however, were not immune to danger either, as buffalo could always break out of the V and trample anyone in their way. When successful, the method resulted in a huge amount of food for the winter months as well as a large quantity of hides.

Another popular approach to hunting buffalo was the two-group surround. Hunters divided into two groups, encircling the herd in two half-circles. From two sides the hunters on horseback charged the buffalo, killing as many as possible. A hunter usually wore only a breechcloth. Clothing flapping in the wind might get in the way of a hand rapidly putting an arrow to the bow string, and bare legs would grip the horse more effectively, pressure from a knee directing the horse because the hunter needed his hands free for shooting. Horses also were stripped of anything that could be discarded, such as a saddle, that might lessen the speed of the specially trained buffalo horses. Old men and young boys followed with the pack horses and helped with the butchering. Some hunters were more skilled than others, and the more successful often shared with the less successful, generosity being an important Lakota virtue.[17]

The Hunkpapas seem to have favored the latter method. It would make them less dependent on terrain and the necessity of locating a suitable cliff nearby, as the buffalo could be taken where they were. The horsemanship and efficiency with the bow and arrow that the two-group surround required also were appealing to a society in which such skills helped determine an individual's social status.

During Hunkesni's initial buffalo hunt, he certainly would not have been among the first line of hunters attacking the buffalo. Nonetheless, he took the opportunity he had and killed a buffalo calf that likely had become separated from the main herd. The accomplishment was not great, certainly not when compared to the mature Sitting Bull's achievements, but it marked the youngster as a hunter. He was on his way to manhood.

THE VISION QUEST

Another milestone for Hunkesni in adolescence was the Vision Quest. No record remains of his participation in this event, but the Vision Quest was of great importance, as significant for the individual as the Sun Dance was for the community. Hunkesni would have approached the ritual with enthusiasm, seeing it as another step toward manhood and finding his place among his people.

At some point, as Hunkesni approached adulthood, most likely in his early teens, he prepared to invite the vision that would help him see into his future and gain both insight and confidence regarding what lay in wait for him. A twenty-first-century adolescent might take aptitude tests, explore career options with a guidance counselor, deliberate about the relative merits of continuing to college after high school or entering the work force. The young Lakota male instead would have embarked on the vision quest.[18]

Preparation was essential and involved self-purification through an *inipi*, or sweat bath, which took place in an *ini ti*, or sweat lodge, under the guidance of a shaman. The sweat lodge consisted of willow saplings stuck into the ground in a circle about six feet in diameter. The tops were bent over and tied to make a dome about four feet high, which was then covered with hides to prevent steam from escaping. One small entrance permitted individuals to crawl into the lodge.

Stones were heated and then carried inside. The entrance was closed, and water was poured over the stones, creating steam and causing anyone inside the lodge to perspire heavily. The perspiration was believed to remove spiritual impurities from the body. After the purification, Hunkesni would have left the lodge, rinsed off with cold water, and set out on his vision quest, probably clothed only in a robe.

Hunkesni would have taken no food or drink, but he certainly carried with him a sacred pipe and cansasa, also known as kinnikinic, which is dried willow or dogwood bark. He probably mixed the cansasa with tobacco in the pipe.

The location was typically an isolated high area where the individual would be completely alone and undisturbed while awaiting the vision. Hunkesni most likely carried with him four charms tied in tiny bundles no larger than a fingertip. He would have placed these spirit banners at the four sides of the spot where he planned to stay, a small plot of land roughly six by three feet. The placing of the charms was to follow a specified pattern, locating the first one toward the west, then toward the north, and, continuing in a clockwise pattern, toward the east and south. Each of the Four Directions was sacred to the Lakotas, and each had its own spirit. Each of the spirits was thus implored for help in securing the anticipated vision.

Hunkesni next would have lit and smoked the pipe, moving it in the same clockwise pattern starting with the west, thus offering the smoke to the spirits residing in the Four Directions. Then Hunkesni would have spent his time not merely waiting but meditating, singing, and imploring the spirits to answer his request. He fasted during his vision quest from both food and water. He might stand, sit, and lie, but he would not leave his small plot of earth until he either received a vision or suffered complete exhaustion.

Hunkesni's quest may have taken several days, but there is no indication that it was unsuccessful. That there is no record of the result is fitting, for the vision was to remain a secret, shared only with the shaman or shamans who had helped prepare the individual for the quest; however, the fact of success was easily discernible. A successful supplicant would return singing; one who had failed to receive a vision would return silently.

The initial vision quest was especially important, but for many Lakotas it would not be the final one. A Lakota, especially a leader, would often embark on a vision quest before any significant undertaking or decision that needed to be made.

Hunkesni's vision, if it were typical of most visions among the Lakotas, was of an animal figure, although it might have been a light, a cloud, or a human figure. Whatever the vision, the experience seemingly helped propel Hunkesni onward to the life that would make him one of the most distinguished Indian leaders in history.

NOTES

1. Stanley Vestal, *Sitting Bull: Champion of the Sioux*, 2nd ed. (1957; Norman: University of Oklahoma Press, 1989), 3; Robert M. Utley, *The Lance and the Shield: The Life and Times of Sitting Bull* (1993; New York: Ballantine Books, 1994), 3.

2. Royal B. Hassrick, *The Sioux: Life and Customs of a Warrior Society* (Norman: University of Oklahoma Press, 1964), 8–11. For a written translation of a winter count, see Iron Shell's Winter Count in Hassrick, 306–11. The count runs from 1807 to 1883 and was begun by Iron Shell's great-grandfather. Iron Shell's son, Arnold Iron Shell, preserved in a notebook a copy of the winter count on which several generations of his ancestors had worked.

3. This overview of the early history of the Sioux is based on Guy Gibbon's *The Sioux: The Dakota and Lakota Nations* (Malden, MA: Blackwell, 2003), 1–6.

4. Utley, 4.

5. Information about Sioux languages is taken from Gibbon, 187–88; Lyle Campbell, *American Indian Languages: The Historical Linguistics of Native America* (New York: Oxford University Press, 1997), 140–42; and Albert Marrin, *Sitting Bull and His World* (New York: Dutton Children's Books, 2000), 11.

6. The information about the Lakota spiritual world presented here is drawn from James R. Walker's *Lakota Belief and Ritual*, ed. Raymond J. DeMallie and Elaine A. Jahner (1980; Lincoln: University of Nebraska Press, 1991), 51, 70–73, 83, 95–96. Walker, a physician on three Indian reservations, including Pine Ridge, based his material on

extensive interviews with elderly Lakota holy men from 1896 to 1914. His research focused on Oglala Lakotas, but culturally there was much similarity between the Oglalas and Hunkpapas, Sitting Bull's tribe. The information that Walker preserved would have been largely representative of the Hunkpapas as well as the Oglalas.

7. See Walker, 50–51, 109–12, 148–50, 295 n.10; and Utley, 30–31, on the story of the giving of the Buffalo Calf Pipe. White Bull notes the incident of confiscation in his winter count, published in *Lakota Warrior*, translated and edited by James H. Howard (1968; Lincoln: University of Nebraska Press, 1998), 24–25. Also see the history of sacred pipes as well as their current use in Tankersley and Pickering's *Sitting Bull's Pipe: Rediscovering the Man, Correcting the Myth* (Wyk, Germany: Tatanka Press, 2006), 85–103.

8. See Walker, 176–93, for detailed accounts of the Sun Dance. Also see Hassrick, 239–48.

9. Vestal, 18.

10. Tom McHugh, *The Time of the Buffalo* (New York: Alfred A. Knopf, 1972), 22, 171.

11. Francis Haines, *The Buffalo* (New York: Thomas Y. Crowell, 1970), 42.

12. McHugh, 88–91, 100; Hassrick, 189.

13. For a discussion of women's role in Lakota culture, see Gibbon, 72–75; and Utley, 6–7.

14. McHugh, 13–17; E. Douglas Branch, *The Hunting of the Buffalo* (1929; Lincoln: University of Nebraska Press), 221–26.

15. Marrin, 24–30, 43. For an extensive study of Indians' uses of, and attitudes toward, horses, see Frank Gilbert Roe, *The Indian and the Horse* (1955; Norman: University of Oklahoma Press, 1962).

16. See Utley, 10; and Marrin, 29–31, 42. For first-hand accounts of games that Lakota boys played, see Luther Standing Bear, *My Indian Boyhood* (1931; Lincoln: University of Nebraska Press, 1988), 131–43; and *My People the Sioux* (1928; Lincoln: University of Nebraska Press, 1975), 28–48.

17. For information on Lakota buffalo hunts, see McHugh, 60–82; and Hassrick, 175–78. Branch throughout his book examines buffalo hunting even more extensively.

18. I am indebted to Walker for information about the vision quest: 84–86, 104–05, 130, 151–53, 295 n.13.

Chapter 2

A WARRIOR TO BE RECKONED WITH (1845–1859)

A WARRIOR SOCIETY

The life of the Lakota male was the life of the warrior, and Hunkesni, like other Lakota boys, looked forward to taking his proper place within the warrior society. Many of the games that he had played as a child helped prepare him for the warrior life, which was, along with hunting, the primary male role.

War was both a necessity and a chosen way of life. Enemies abounded, but war also provided the means whereby a Lakota male could earn his status as a respected member of his people. Hunkesni did not wait long before embarking on this way of life, counting his first coup at the age of 14 in 1845. To understand Hunkesni's actions satisfactorily, it is necessary to understand in some depth the function of war within the Lakota society.

Hunkesni's Hunkpapa tribe had many enemies among the Plains Indians, chiefly the Crows to the west and the Assiniboines farther north. Many other tribes less close in proximity to the Hunkpapas also were adversaries, some of which, such as the Arikara, Mandan, and Hidatsa (also known as Gros Ventres), were no longer serious rivals. These three tribes in particular had suffered so severely the effects of smallpox, contracted from European settlers, that their population had sharply declined, making them less able to compete with the Lakotas. In 1837, for example, Euroamericans aboard a steamboat brought smallpox to several tribes along the Missouri River. The tribes most affected by imported diseases lived in earth-lodge villages along the river, their sedentary lifestyle making them susceptible to the white man's illnesses that the more mobile Lakotas were less likely to contract.[1]

Two previously formidable enemies, the Cheyenne and Arapaho tribes, had become Lakota allies by the time Hunkesni met his first enemy in battle. In fact, Cheyennes, along with a handful of Arapahos, were with the Lakotas at the Battle of the Little Bighorn in 1876. At the same battle, two of the traditional enemies of the Lakotas, the Crows and Arikaras, supplied the cavalry with most of its scouts, or *wolves*, the term Indians used for army scouts.[2]

Seldom did Indian tribes fight each other in large-scale battles. Except in self-defense or to revenge an especially atrocious action, Lakotas fought their enemies in small war parties and for two primary purposes: (1) to establish their own warrior credentials, earn fame among their people, and advance to leadership positions in the tribe; and (2) to gain horses. The great importance of the horse in Lakota society is discussed in Chapter 1.

A typical raiding party consisted of five to ten men, who prepared themselves by stripping away their clothes except for breechcloth and moccasins and painting their bodies and war horses. Many warriors rode their regular horses until it was time for the battle, when they switched to faster horses trained to work better in combat. The "war paint" was not to frighten fainthearted enemies but to secure spiritual power. Painted symbols represented past accomplishments; for example, straight lines on the horse denoted the warrior's number of coups, and painted hoof prints on the horse represented horse-stealing raids. Painting oneself and wearing ornaments in battle also were a matter of dressing up for what might be the most significant event in the warrior's life—his death. Lakotas, like many other tribes, believed that when they died they would enter the spirit world looking as they did in this world, and they wanted to look their best for that all-important journey.

The warrior would be well armed, quite likely with a bow and arrows, lance, coup stick, knife, tomahawk (essentially a hatchet), and war club (a wooden handle supporting a stone attached with rawhide). If available, a rifle added to the warrior's firepower. A shield made from buffalo hide shrunken over heat until it was hard and as thick as a man's finger offered good protection from arrows but did not prove effective against bullets, as Hunkesni would discover at a later battle. Because of its protective function, the shield was believed to possess supernatural power and was adorned with designs connected with the spiritual world, perhaps an image that had come to the owner in a dream.

Scouts often preceded the rest of the party. Covered in wolf skins, a scout could lie undetected on high ground while examining all directions.

If he saw no enemies, he would continue; if he sighted his quarry, he would return with the message or signal the rest by waving a blanket or riding his horse in a particular pattern.

Because personal honor came before killing the enemy, Lakota warriors favored individual hand-to-hand combat. Touching the enemy was considered more courageous than killing him at a distance, hence the importance of counting coup, often with a coup stick, a peeled stick with a feather tied to it. Lakota war practice permitted four people to count coup on a single enemy, but first coup was the most important. Killing the enemy was much further down the line of honors, and the person who counted first coup often would leave the killing to others.

In warfare, generally no distinction was made between combatants and noncombatants. Women and children were subject to death and dismemberment as well as the men. Sitting Bull's first pictographic autobiography, a series of drawings he completed in 1870, begins with a depiction of Sitting Bull's first coup in 1846 and includes pictures of Sitting Bull killing women in battle.[3] To kill a woman in the presence of her husband was viewed as a particular act of courage. Dismemberment, such as removing the enemy's scalp or another part of the body, was done to ensure that the enemy would continue to suffer in the afterlife, where his disfigurement would be permanent.

The Lakota culture was an oral society. Although winter counts, ledger books (pictures of exploits drawn in ledger books normally used by white businessmen to record revenue and expenses),[4] and other visual representations recorded important historical moments, it was left to the oral tradition to convey detailed accounts of memorable individual accomplishments. Performing heroic actions brought the sort of esteem that would be talked about in the village at night, perhaps even, if the exploits were memorable enough, by future generations.[5]

Thus individual heroism often took precedence over collective action. So long as enemies existed, the opportunities for individual heroism remained, and a variety of forces conspired to prevent any extensive peace among the Plains Indians. Guy Gibbon, in *The Sioux: The Dakota and Lakota Nations*, has enumerated these "historic causes" of intertribal warfare with great thoroughness:

> (1) the migration into the Plains of Indian groups from both east and west, and the displacement of resident tribes; (2) the westward movement of the Euro-American frontier, which forced eastern tribes into the Plains; (3) the unequal possession of firearms among tribes, which led to an imbalance of

power; (4) the desire for horses; (5) competition for good hunting grounds; (6) the territorial shrinkage of the bison herds; (7) protection of markets; (8) the machinations of traders and government agents; (9) epidemics, which weakened some once powerful tribes and made them easy prey for the Sioux and other less affected foe; (10) the warfare-revenge cycle; (11) the importance of warfare to young men as an avenue to sociopolitical positions; and (12) tribal ethnocentrism, which resulted in feelings of hostility toward outsiders ("aliens").[6]

All of these factors created a warlike society that endured until a more powerful enemy, the Euroamerican, forced the tribes into peaceful coexistence on reservations, at the cost of the tribes' freedom and much of their traditional way of life. Until that time, the young warrior put these historical forces to use to advance himself within his own tribal society.

FIRST COUP

So it was that the 14-year-old Hunkesni was waiting impatiently for his first encounter with the enemy. That occurred when a group of Hunkpapas moved into Crow territory and camped on the Powder River in the southeastern portion of the present state of Montana. A war party of about 10 warriors was established and proceeded to set out on a raid against their Crow enemies. Hunkesni decided to join them.

In preparation, Hunkesni painted his body yellow and his horse red, colors believed to be pleasing to the spirits.[7] Hunkesni rode a particularly fast gray horse that his father, at the time still known as Sitting Bull, had given him. The war party came upon about a dozen Crows, and the Hunkpapas attacked. Details of what happened next vary, including whether most of the Crows took up defensive positions, or whether they all tried to race their horses away.[8] At least one Crow, however, turned his horse and fled, with Hunkesni in pursuit.

Spurring his gray on, Hunkesni quickly caught up with the fleeing Crow. Accounts also differ as to whether Hunkesni knocked the Crow off his horse or whether, seeing his pursuer gaining, the Crow jumped off his horse in preparation for battle. The latter version corresponds more precisely to the pictographic account of the engagement that Hunkesni, by then renamed Sitting Bull, drew in 1870.[9] In that drawing, Hunkesni is mounted and ready to strike with a coup stick a Crow who stands on the ground preparing to shoot an arrow at his mounted adversary. In these drawings, Sitting Bull signs his art work with a small picture of a sitting buffalo suspended in the upper right corner of the page and connected to Sitting Bull's mouth by a curving line. The young mounted warrior wears no eagle feathers in his hair, having not yet earned any. He apparently struck the Crow with his coup stick, causing the arrow to go astray, thus counting first coup. Hunkesni's horse then knocked the man to the ground, and another Hunkpapa killed him. From the drawing as well as written accounts, Hunkesni likely did not carry any weapon with him into battle except for the coup stick.

Hunkesni's first coup was a major achievement for the adolescent and marked his entry into the warrior way of life. His father led a public celebration of his son's courage. He gave Hunkesni his first eagle feather, placing it in his hair. In an act of generosity typical of Lakotas, he gave away horses to four less affluent tribesmen, painted his son black as a sign of victory, and led his son mounted on horseback in a sort of victory lap among the tipis.

Sitting Bull also gave Hunkesni a shield and lance. On the shield was a dark birdlike figure, resembling a stylized eagle or perhaps a type of bird-man, that had appeared to the father in a dream. A holy man had painted the figure on the shield, and the son instantly recognized the mystical and protective nature of the image. Four eagle feathers stretched from the shield toward the four directions, symbolizing future success for the son regardless of the direction or endeavor that he pursued. Throughout his life, the adult Sitting Bull carried the shield with him, and it often appears in his pictographic scenes.

The lance was about seven or eight feet long, with a shaft made of ash, an iron blade, and an eagle feather at its base. His mother, Her Holy Door, decorated the lance with blue and white beads. When not in use, the lance was protected in a special case. The lance quickly became a favorite weapon of the great Lakota warrior. As with the shield, the pictographs regularly show the lance in combat.[10]

Also of lasting importance was the new name that Sitting Bull conferred on his son. He gave Hunkesni his own name, Tatanka-Iyotanka, or Sitting Bull, assuming as a replacement for himself the name Jumping Bull.[11]

The renaming of Hunkesni and the father's assumption of the name Jumping Bull followed a pattern the father had earlier encountered in a vision. As the story goes, Jumping Bull, then known as Returns Again, and three companions were sitting around a campfire when they heard someone approaching.[12] The visitor proved to be a large buffalo. Fortunately, Returns Again possessed the ability to understand what animals were saying.

While the other men stood motionless in fear, Returns Again listened to the buffalo, which he took to be the buffalo god worshipped in the Sun Dance, utter a sequence of four names: Sitting Bull, Jumping Bull, Bull Standing with Cow, and Lone Bull. Returns Again understood the four names to represent the four ages of people: infancy, youth, maturity (the name representing a married couple), and old age (the person left alone after his companion's death). The buffalo god was seemingly offering Returns Again four names.

After this incident, Returns Again abandoned his original name and adopted Sitting Bull. Therefore, in passing his name on to Hunkesni, he was taking for himself the second name given by the buffalo. Jumping Bull would later also use the final two names, giving them to the two sons of his daughter Good Feather. The elder of the two grandsons later adopted the name Big in the Center as a replacement for Bull Standing with Cow and also became known, more commonly, as White Bull. Lone Bull (or One Bull, as Utley translates the name) retained his name and was adopted by his uncle, Sitting Bull.[13] One Bull later fought at the Battle of Little Bighorn.

The younger Sitting Bull inherited not only his name from his father but also apparently the ability to interpret what animals were saying. Sitting Bull's life is filled with examples of animals, especially birds, seemingly communicating with him. The examples range from a warning in his youth by a yellowhammer to lie still to avoid an attack by a grizzly bear[14] to a meadowlark's prophecy near the end of his life that Sitting Bull would die at the hands of his own people, a prophecy that came true.[15]

EARLY BATTLES

In the meantime, however, the newly renamed Sitting Bull had much to accomplish, although those accomplishments often came with a price. About a year after his first coup, Sitting Bull suffered his first wound in combat. A band of Sitting Bull's Hunkpapas was camping along the Musselshell River above the Yellowstone in present-day Montana when Hunkpapa scouts reported enemy Flatheads nearby. About 15 Hunkpapas, including Sitting Bull, responded to the alert and were ambushed by approximately 20 Flatheads.

When the Flatheads dismounted and formed a line, firing at the Hunkpapas, Sitting Bull raced his horse down the entire line in a demonstration of his courage, daring the enemy to hit him. One did, wounding Sitting Bull slightly in a foot, but after the battle there could be little doubt about the teenager's bravery. The Flatheads eventually withdrew, leaving the

Hunkpapas to celebrate their victory. In addition to his people's acclaim, Sitting Bull received a red feather, a symbol of his having been wounded in battle, akin to the Purple Heart awarded current U.S. military personnel in recognition of battle wounds.

Sitting Bull was impressive in appearance as well as in deed. He stood about 5 feet 10 inches in height, a reasonably tall man for that time. He had a muscular body with an especially large chest.[16] Sitting Bull was known as a strong swimmer and fast runner, activities that helped him develop his physical form and endurance.

Another early encounter that contributed to Sitting Bull's growing renown as a warrior occurred in 1851, shortly after his marriage to Light Hair.[17] The two had gone on a hunting expedition and were camped on Powder River. The hunt had gone well, so successfully that Sitting Bull had used up most of his arrows. He was sitting inside their tipi fashioning new arrows, with Light Hair working over a cook fire when she saw a reflection of an enemy Crow who had climbed a nearby tree and was peering down through the smoke opening in the tipi. Light Hair whispered a warning to her husband, who grabbed his bow and shot an arrow through the vent. He dashed outside but could not catch the escaping Crow. A blood track, however, showed that he had at least wounded his opponent.

Sitting Bull suffered a second, more serious wound, in 1856. Both Vestal and Utley discuss the incident in detail.[18] Sitting Bull and a number of other Hunkpapas entered a Crow camp and stole a large number of horses. Driving the horses slowed them down, however, and by sunrise a large body of Crows had caught up to them. Although some Hunkpapas kept the captured horses under control, the rest lined up ready to meet the Crow charge. Instead, the Crows stopped short, reconsidering whether they wanted to charge into a waiting group of Hunkpapa warriors. Only three Crow leaders came forward, and Sitting Bull advanced to meet one of them.

Both Sitting Bull and the Crow dismounted and approached each other, both men armed with flintlock muskets. The Crow fired first, his bullet striking the shield that Sitting Bull's father had given him. Made of layers of buffalo hide, the shield, although effective against arrows, could not completely stop bullets. The shield partly deflected the bullet, however, altering its trajectory, so that it angled downward and hit Sitting Bull in his left foot. The bullet struck just below Sitting Bull's toes and carved a canal down his sole to the heel.

Sitting Bull also fired, his bullet hitting the Crow in the stomach. Limping to the Crow, Sitting Bull stabbed him and then removed his scalp. The wound left Sitting Bull with a permanent limp but added another red feather to the man who by this time was widely accepted as a great Lakota warrior and leader.

Sitting Bull's first pictographic autobiography includes a representation of this encounter with the Crow.[19] The picture depicts the two adversaries, Sitting Bull's horse in the background, with Sitting Bull kneeling to protect as much of his body as possible behind the shield, his left foot, which would take the brunt of the attack, stretching outward unprotected. Both guns are spraying shot, as Sitting Bull and other Indian artists regularly used multiple lines from a gun's muzzle to the enemy to illustrate shooting. In fact, only one bullet was fired by each of the two combatants.

Sitting Bull, previously named one of the two sash bearers in the Strong Heart Society because of his military accomplishments, is wearing the headdress (a skullcap with two sharp buffalo horns and short crow feathers) and sash of the society. The sash was a long strip of scarlet cloth with a slit at one end permitting an arm to go through it so that the sash could be worn over a shoulder. The other end of the sash was staked to the ground with a picket pin; the warrior stood in place until he killed his enemy, was himself killed, or was released by a fellow warrior.

RISE TO LEADERSHIP

As a young man, Sitting Bull became a member of the Strong Heart and Kit Fox Societies, both prestigious akicita societies, that is, fraternal military organizations open only to the most successful warriors, and from which akicitas, individuals whose responsibilities included enforcing tribal regulations, were drawn. Membership in such societies was crucial to attaining tribal leadership positions.[20]

Sitting Bull and two other Hunkpapa leaders, Crow King and Gall, created an even more elite group out of the Strong Heart Society—the Midnight Strong Heart Society. It is not known precisely why they added the concept of midnight to the name, although Vestal conjectures that it may have been because they conducted their meetings at midnight or did their fighting then. It is known that some societies, such as the Silent Eaters, a men's society in which Sitting Bull later became heavily involved, met at midnight.[21] The midnight reference may also have related to values exhibited by the members such as absolute dedication and courage, as midnight represents the ultimate in darkness, or it may simply connote a sense of mystery.

Regardless of the symbolic reference, Sitting Bull was quickly becoming a special leader. His pictographic autobiography records a number of battles during the 1850s, with Crows the most common enemy, although in Illustration 8, he counts coup on an enemy variously identified as a Gros Ventre or Hohe (the latter tribe also known as Assiniboines).[22]

If Vestal is correct in stating that the incident in Illustration 8 involves the boy that Sitting Bull saved and adopted as his brother, the year would have been 1857, an especially noteworthy year in Sitting Bull's life. In that year, the Midnight Strong Heart Society made him a war chief, an honor that certainly helped lead to an even higher position when he was selected as a war chief of his tribe. Recommendations for positions were as important then as they are now, and the recommendations on behalf of Sitting Bull to become a Hunkpapa chief came from four of his close associates, including Gall, with whom Sitting Bull had formed the Midnight Strong Heart Society.[23]

Sitting Bull and Gall continued as close friends and fellow warriors for years, fighting together at Little Bighorn and in other battles throughout the 1860s and 1870s. During the 1880s, however, as Euroamericans increasingly restricted the freedom of the Plains Indians, Gall's efforts to accommodate the newcomers' directives and secure peace resulted in growing estrangement between the old friends.[24]

Sitting Bull's Strong Heart position included responsibility for hunting, a function closely related to war in Lakota society. With buffalo decreasing in numbers as Euroamericans increased their pursuit of the animal, expanded hunting grounds were necessary to provide for the tribe's needs. That took the Hunkpapas and other Lakota tribes into enemy territory. The Crows, Mandans, Hidatsas, Hohes, Shoshones, and other tribes had the same need for the buffalo as the Lakotas, but superior Lakota numbers and the skill of such leaders as Sitting Bull made resistance largely futile. Many tribes quickly pulled away from their traditional homes, some even offering their hereditary lands for sale to the U.S. government, arguing that they were unable to use their lands because of the Lakotas.[25]

SITTING BULL'S PERSONAL LIFE

In addition to Sitting Bull's new responsibilities, the year included major changes in his personal life. Sitting Bull's first wife, Light Hair, had died giving birth to a son. Then, in 1857, at the age of four, the boy died. The loss had the expected result, causing great grief for Sitting Bull. To help assuage his sorrow and establish a son to carry on as a direct descendant, Sitting Bull adopted his nephew, One Bull (Lone Bull), son of Good Feather and a Miniconjou chief, Makes Room. The Miniconjou tribe was another division of the Lakotas and thus closely allied socially and militarily with the Hunkpapas. One Bull's elder brother, White Bull, remained with the Miniconjous. The two brothers lived into their nineties, each dying in 1947, and in later years they provided detailed information about their famous uncle.[26]

Although much about Sitting Bull's personal life remains uncertain, including his wives, before the deaths of his first wife and his natural son, he apparently had taken a second wife named Snow on Her. Having multiple wives was commonplace among the Lakotas, in part because so many men died in war that women outnumbered them and, without the convention of multiple wives, would have had to live alone. Yet the second wife quarreled extensively with Light Hair, seemingly out of jealousy.

Snow on Her told lies about Light Hair, claiming, for instance, that Sitting Bull's first wife was unfaithful to him. Vestal describes how Light Hair sought the help of a highly respected older woman to verify her own faithfulness. The elderly woman summoned the women who claimed to have only one man and then inquired of the men in the camp whether any of them had been intimate with these women. If so, the man was to pick up a gun, knife, or arrow that had been placed in a shallow hole and kill the woman who had lied. No man came forward, and Light Hair, as well as the other women, was vindicated. At the same time, Snow on Her was proven to be lying, and Sitting Bull sent her home to her parents.

Utley offers a different chronology for the wives, stating that Sitting Bull married Snow on Her, as well as a woman named Red Woman, after Light Hair's death. He describes the conflict as occurring between the two later wives rather than between Light Hair and Snow on Her but also makes Snow on Her the villain in the story and the wife rejected by Sitting Bull, although not until the late 1860s. According to Utley, Sitting Bull had two daughters by Snow on Her and a son by Red Woman.[27]

Sitting Bull added another adopted family member in 1857 during a battle with Hohes north of the Missouri River in present-day Montana. A Hunkpapa raiding party attacked a group of Hohes and pursued them across a shallow lake. A number of the Hohes reached the other side and escaped into the woods, but a Hohe family was not so fortunate.

Sitting Bull's fellow warriors brought a youthful captive to him, the only survivor of the family, his parents and two brothers having been killed in the encounter. As the Hunkpapas prepared to kill the boy, who despite being only about 11 years old had bravely fought with his bow and arrows, he called out to Sitting Bull for protection, hugged him, and called him his "older brother." No doubt affected by the death of his own son, and perhaps by the boy's courage, Sitting Bull granted him his life over the strong objections of other members of the Hunkpapa party, especially Swift Cloud, who had counted first coup on the boy.[28]

Sitting Bull decided to adopt the Hohe (or Assiniboine) youngster as his brother, although many Hunkpapas opposed his decision. Among those in opposition was another war chief, No Neck, the leader of a group generally opposing Sitting Bull, who, although widely popular, was not loved by everyone.[29] The Hunkpapas generally referred to their new tribesman by the name Stays Back because, even when given the opportunity to return to the Hohes, he chose to stay back with Sitting Bull. He also earned the name Kills Plenty for his war exploits. The adoption later bore political fruit when it helped lead to a truce between the Lakotas and Hohes.

The decade of the 1850s, during which Sitting Bull rose to leadership among the Hunkpapas and renown among the various tribes of Plains Indians, was a time of both great accomplishments and great sorrows for Sitting Bull. One of the latter was still to come.

DEATH OF SITTING BULL'S FATHER

In the spring of 1859, Sitting Bull; his father, Jumping Bull; and other Hunkpapas camped on the Cannonball River in Slope County, in Dakota Territory, and had just started moving north in the morning when a large group of Crows attacked. Two Hunkpapa boys had strayed off from the rest of the party and one was quickly cut down. The Hunkpapa and Crow warriors engaged in a number of individual battles while other Crows fled with Hunkpapas in pursuit. One of the Crows found himself afoot when his horse went down, and Hunkpapas quickly surrounded him.

Jumping Bull, who had suffered much the night before from a toothache, called to his men to leave the Crow to him. Much has been made of the toothache inducing some sort of death wish, but it is unlikely that an ailing tooth in itself rendered the chief, by now in his sixties, tired of life. It may, however, have been just one more sign of his advancing age and declining physical strength in a culture that made participation in war an integral part of what it meant to be a man.

Perhaps resolving to reassert his masculinity and sense of self-worth or die in the attempt, Jumping Bull dismounted and engaged the Crow in one-on-one combat. The Crow came at Jumping Bull with his knife, and when the aging chief tried to pull out his own knife, he found that his sheath had slid behind his back where he could not quickly reach it. The Crow rammed his knife into Jumping Bull's neck and cut downward, ripping his chest open. He then withdrew the knife and plunged it downward into Jumping Bull's head, breaking the knife off in his skull.[30]

In another version of Jumping Bull's final battle, the Crow waits on horseback until he sees Jumping Bull approaching, then dismounts and shoots the Lakota in a shoulder. From that point on, the account is similar to the other version except that the Crow stabs Jumping Bull several times in the chest.[31]

The Crow tried to flee, but Sitting Bull, informed of what had just occurred, raced his horse after his father's killer and knocked him off his feet with his lance, a scene depicted in Illustration 9 of the first pictographic autobiography. A circle of Hunkpapas then surrounded the Crow and shot him with arrows and musket balls. Sitting Bull jumped from his horse and repeatedly stabbed the Crow with his knife. Sitting Bull, filled with rage at his father's death, pursued the Crows and killed several before his own men managed to persuade him to return, fearing that in his frenzy he would recklessly endanger himself.

The immediate aftermath of this incident demonstrates Sitting Bull's ability to reclaim self-control even after what surely was one of the most traumatic events of his life. The fleeing Crows had left behind three Crow women and a male baby. Sitting Bull's men wanted to kill the four in revenge for Jumping Bull's death. Sitting Bull instead reminded his tribesmen that his father was a great warrior, and such men should die in battle. "If you intend to do this for my sake, take good care of them and let them live," he is reported as saying. "My father is a man and death is his."[32] With Jumping Bull dead, Sitting Bull transferred his father's name to his own adopted brother, the Hohe Stays Back, an act that conferred great honor on the boy.

The battles that Sitting Bull waged during the 1850s were with other Indian tribes, the natural enemies of the Lakotas. Sitting Bull had no natural antipathy toward Euroamericans, and it was in combat with other Indians that a young Lakota would traditionally earn his status within his own people. In the next decade, however, the concept of warfare for the Lakotas would broaden dramatically as a new enemy arose.

NOTES

1. Jeffrey Ostler, *The Plains Sioux and U.S. Colonialism from Lewis and Clark to Wounded Knee* (New York: Cambridge University Press, 2004), 22.

2. Mark L. Gardner, *Little Bighorn Battlefield National Monument* (Tucson: Western National Parks Association, 2005), 5–6.

3. Sitting Bull's first pictographic autobiography is known as *The Kimball Pictographic Record* after the physician, Dr. James Kimball, who acquired a copy of the original drawings in 1870. The series is published in *Three Pictographic Autobiographies of Sitting Bull*, edited by M. W. Stirling (Washington, DC: Smithsonian Institution, 1938). See, for example, Illustrations 2 and 4.

4. Several original ledger books, and much information about the genre, can be viewed online at The Plains Indian Ledger Art site <www.plainsledgerart.org>.

5. Many of the war details given here are drawn from Stanley Vestal, *Sitting Bull: Champion of the Sioux*, 2nd ed. (1957; Norman: University of Oklahoma Press, 1989), 9–11; Robert M. Utley, *The Lance and the Shield: The Life and Times of Sitting Bull* (1993; New York: Ballantine Books, 1994), 16–17; Guy Gibbon, *The Sioux: The Dakota and Lakota Nations* (Malden, MA: Blackwell, 2003), 87–89; and Albert Marrin, *Sitting Bull and His World* (New York: Dutton Children's Books, 2000), 43–48.

6. Gibbon, 93–94.

7. James R. Walker, *Lakota Belief and Ritual*, ed. Raymond J. DeMallie and Elaine A. Jahner (1980; Lincoln: University of Nebraska Press, 1991), 108.

8. See the accounts by Vestal, Sitting Bull, 11–12; and Utley, 14.

9. See Illustration 1.

10. See, for example, Illustrations 2–5, 7, 9, 10.

11. Vestal, Sitting Bull, 12–13; and Utley, 14–15; describe Jumping Bull's celebration for his son. For a detailed, step-by-step description of how Jumping Bull made the shield, see Stanley Vestal, *New Sources of Indian History 1850–1891* (Norman: University of Oklahoma Press, 1934), 152–56.

12. Vestal, Sitting Bull, 15–17.

13. Utley, 23.

14. Vestal, Sitting Bull, 20–21.

15. Utley, 290.

16. Utley, 19.

17. For the controversy surrounding Light Hair's name, see Utley, 20.

18. Vestal, Sitting Bull, 27–30; Utley, 21.

19. See Illustration 6.

20. Utley, 16–18. For additional information about the roles of an akicita, see James R. Walker, *Lakota Society*, ed. Raymond J. DeMallie (Lincoln: University of Nebraska Press, 1982), 28–29 and 32–34.

21. Vestal, *Sitting Bull*, 30; Utley 101.

22. The Kimball Pictographic Record, p. 11.

23. Utley, 22.

24. For discussions of Gall, see Robert W. Larson, "Gall: 'The Fighting Cock of the Sioux,'" *Wild West*, June 2006, 26–32; and Gall: *Lakota Sioux War Chief* (Norman: University of Oklahoma Press, 2007).

25. Vestal, *Sitting Bull*, 31–33.

26. Utley, 22–23.

27. Vestal, *Sitting Bull*, 39–41; Utley, 70, 100.

28. Vestal, *Sitting Bull*, 34–36; Utley, 23.

29. Vestal, *Sitting Bull*, 36.

30. Most of the account given here comes from Utley, 24–25.

31. Vestal, *Sitting Bull*, 45–49.

32. Utley, 25.

Chapter 3

THE HOLY MAN VERSUS THE U.S. GOVERNMENT (1851–1867)

WICHASHA WAKAN

Sitting Bull excelled as a warrior and hunter, but at least as important to his role as a leader was his status as a Wichasha Wakan, that is, a holy man or shaman. Wakan referred to the spiritual or mysterious in life and made up the first part of the name of Wakantanka, the Great Mystery, the divine being that included all spirits or gods within itself. The term *wichasha* meant *man*. Consequently, to call someone a Wichasha Wakan meant that the individual was an especially holy or spiritual person.

The term *Wichasha Wakan* was not applied lightly, the way someone today might casually refer to a man or woman as a good person or a religious person. Wichasha Wakan was a title that one had to earn through a variety of endeavors, not least of which was to suffer greatly at the Sun Dance. Sitting Bull participated in the Sun Dance when he was in his mid-twenties, choosing the most painful version of the dance. He hung suspended from the pole, hooks inserted under the skin of his chest and back until the skin finally gave way. While hanging, he prayed aloud to Wakantanka for the well-being of his people. Sitting Bull claimed, and no doubt believed, that Wakantanka spoke to him, promising that he would answer his prayers. According to his nephew One Bull, Sitting Bull often danced the Sun Dance after that to secure the safety and health of his tribe.[1]

A Wichasha Wakan spoke for Wakantanka and had to possess a wide range of abilities. According to Little Wound, an Oglala chief:

> A *wakan* man is one who is wise. It is one who knows the spirits. It is one who has power with the spirits. It is one who communicates with the spirits. It is one who can do strange things. A *wakan* man knows things that the people do not know. He knows the ceremonies and the songs. He can tell the people what their visions mean. He can tell the people what the spirits wish them to do. He can tell what is to be in the future. He can talk with animals and with trees and with stones. He can talk with everything on earth.[2]

Sitting Bull was widely acknowledged to possess all of these attributes. Sitting Bull told a journalist for the *New York Herald* in 1877 that he was given the power to see and understand even while he was in his mother's womb. He believed that during this prenatal stage he was empowered by Wakantanka to be the judge and leader for all other Indians. As indicated in Chapter 1, no record remains of Sitting Bull's vision quest, which he surely concluded in adolescence; however, he undoubtedly received directions at that time reaffirming his sense of purpose.

Visions and dreams remained important to Sitting Bull, as they were generally to the Lakotas. Unlike visions, which were the culmination of a set of rituals, dreams came spontaneously, as they apparently did often enough to Sitting Bull so that he became prominent in a number of dream societies, which were much like the akicita societies. Sitting Bull was especially active in the Buffalo Society and the Heyoka, the latter an organization for those who dreamed of the Thunder Bird, or Wakinyan. This winged god was believed to reside in the West, where all animals were thought to have been created and where the revered eagle supposedly had its original home. The Thunder Bird was believed to cause thunder, and its eyes radiated lightening. Given the relationship of lightning storms to rain, it is not surprising that Lakotas saw the Thunder Bird as controller of the weather and thus of extreme importance.[3]

Members of the Heyoka organization were known as singers and healers.[4] Sitting Bull certainly satisfied both of those criteria. He was much respected among his people for his singing and was reported to have a wide repertory of songs depending on the occasion. According to his nephews, One Bull and White Bull, as well as other members of his tribe, many of his songs were spiritual in nature, sung during a particular religious ceremony. Others were secular, such as a song in tribute to his mother, Her Holy Door. Sitting Bull also sang of his love for children, in preparation for battle and in celebration of animals and birds.[5]

Sitting Bull not only respected animals but believed that he could communicate with them, especially with birds. Testimony from Hunkpapas who knew him well make it clear that Sitting Bull was thoroughly sincere in his belief that he could speak with animals.[6] This gift, however, was not seen as unique to Sitting Bull, but as a trait generally associated with a Wichasha Wakan.

Sitting Bull was not a medicine man, but he was skilled in healing, another trait associated with a Heyoka member and certainly a quality that enhanced his standing as a Wichasha Wakan. One of the most prominent examples of his healing abilities came in the aftermath of the Battle of Little Bighorn in 1876, when he tended to an ankle wound that White Bull had suffered. Twelve years earlier, on July 28, 1864, he had administered to the wounds that his uncle Four Horns suffered at the Battle of Killdeer Mountain.[7]

Explaining visions and interpreting the directives of Wakantanka were crucial roles for a Wichasha Wakan, and Sitting Bull was highly respected when he spoke of such matters. Possibly his most famous visions, which are discussed in Chapter 6, occurred in the lead-up to the defeat of Colonel Custer at the Little Bighorn. Sitting Bull, as a conduit for Wakantanka, did not believe that he had to argue or persuade his people to accept what he had seen and heard. Speaking should be enough, given the divine origins of what he said at those times. That attitude comes through clearly in the *New York Herald* interview in which Sitting Bull recalled his prenatal enlightenment and his calling to decide for his people. "'And you have since decided for them?'" the reporter asked Sitting Bull. His response: "'I speak. It is enough.'"[8]

Sitting Bull's acclaim as a holy man, as well as a warrior and hunter, meant that he had excelled in all of the major public areas of importance to the Lakotas. Yet he also was renowned for his personal characteristics. Sitting Bull was extraordinarily generous, regularly giving away his possessions, including innumerable horses, to family, friends, and simply those in need. His pictographic autobiographies record a number of horses or mules that he captured and then gave away to one of his sisters.[9] Another pictograph, number 31, depicts Sitting Bull capturing a horse that he gave to his adopted brother, Jumping Bull. Sitting Bull was given to collective generosity as much as to acts of kindness toward individuals. In March 1876, for example, a cavalry attack on a village of Northern Cheyennes, Oglalas, and Miniconjous resulted in the destruction of much of the village. Although casualties were light, the survivors faced winter weather with little food or means of keeping warm. They made their way 60 miles to Sitting Bull's camp, to be received with kettles of meat, gifts of robes and blankets, and even horses and tipis.[10]

Sitting Bull, as all great leaders should, cared deeply about the people he led. Not only did he willingly suffer great pain during the Sun Dance for their welfare, but he consistently watched out for them, praying to

Wakantanka for food and trying to safeguard his warriors in battle. Many times he pulled his men out of conflicts because he feared for their safety. White Bull recalled an occasion around 1871 when he and other young men were circling U.S. soldiers, with a number of the warriors being hit. Sitting Bull vociferously ordered them to withdraw, noting that too many were being wounded. Similar examples of his concern for his men can be drawn from other battles, such as the conflict of August 1864, with General Alfred Sully's forces when, recognizing how hungry and badly armed his warriors were, he urged them to withdraw.[11]

Sitting Bull's concern for his Hunkpapa tribe led him about 1869 to become a major force in the Silent Eaters. He may even have created the society. Like many Lakota societies, the Silent Eaters was a secret group. Members met at midnight, each meeting containing a strong spiritual component and ending with a pipe ceremony. Their dining was done without song and dance, hence the organization's name. The focus of the organization was neither war, socializing, nor dreams, but the welfare of the community; members discussed problems that the Hunkpapa community faced, for example, hunger or individual personal problems, and devised solutions. The Silent Eaters were so respected that the chiefs usually accepted their proposals.[12]

Sitting Bull, possessor of such a wide range of virtues, also practiced humility. He usually dressed simply, spoke quietly and judiciously but inevitably with authority, was renowned for being a "good listener," and gave away many of his possessions. A rare indulgence was a large tipi that exhibited painted scenes of his achievements. His biographer Robert Utley summed up Sitting Bull's virtues succinctly and effectively:

> As Sitting Bull added honor after honor to his war record and achieved ever greater fame as a *Wichasha Wakan*, he emerged as the Hunkpapa incarnate, epitome of the four cardinal virtues of bravery, fortitude, generosity, and wisdom.[13]

WESTWARD EXPANSION

Sitting Bull's extensive personal accomplishments and talents, as well as his status as a Wichasha Wakan, made him an ideal leader. That leadership would be tested many times in conflicts, not only with other tribes but with Euroamericans, both official representatives of the U.S. government, including soldiers, and civilians moving westward across the traditional domain of the Lakotas.

Much had transpired since Sitting Bull was born around 1831. At that time, the population of the United States numbered about 13 million, roughly 9 million of them Euroamericans and fewer than 3,000 Hunkpapas. The Hunkpapas lived and hunted on approximately 50,000 square miles of the U.S. total of 1.8 million square miles. As Sitting Bull reached the age of 20, the United States had extended its borders to the Pacific Ocean, with the country comprising 3 million square miles and numbering 23.2 million people within its borders. The Hunkpapa population and range, however, remained largely unchanged, although both figures would soon shrink.[14]

A variety of forces had enabled the Euroamerican thrust westward into and across the traditional homes of American Indian tribes. The famous Lewis and Clark expedition, led by Meriwether Lewis and William Clark from 1804 to 1806, had helped to establish the Pacific Ocean as the westernmost boundary of the United States. The U.S. President during the Lewis and Clark expedition, Thomas Jefferson, believed in westward expansion but hoped to induce Indian tribes to accept peacefully the westward movement of the descendents of Europe. Jefferson proposed, in a message to Congress on January 18, 1803, the carrot of commerce, suggesting that trading would "place within their reach those things which will contribute more to their domestic comfort than the possession of extensive, but uncultivated wilds. Experience & reflection," he argued, "will develop to them the wisdom of exchanging what they can spare & we want, for what we can spare and they want." Their choosing farming over hunting, Jefferson realized, would free up considerable land, although Jefferson assured Congress that in pursuing these strategies, "I trust and believe we are acting for their greatest good."[15] When Sitting Bull was born, however, Andrew Jackson was president and he established a new policy toward Indians, one that shelved efforts at economic inducement in favor of abrogating treaties and using force. By supporting efforts of the state of Georgia to expel Indians from territory to which they were entitled by treaty, Jackson set in motion an approach that Sitting Bull and virtually every other Indian leader would face in the coming decades.

Technological developments made it possible for eastern farmers to view the Plains, previously considered desert, as land just waiting to be put to the plow. And John Deere had given farmers the means by which they could turn up the soil that in the past had clung to cast-iron plows, requiring regular pausing to clean off the share (the portion that cuts into the earth) and thus making plowing large tracts of land virtually impossible. Deere, a former blacksmith, redesigned the share in the 1830s and made it out of polished steel, which cut through the ground without soil sticking to it like cement. Another inventor, Cyrus McCormick, developed a reaper that could separate grain from straw. He gave his first public demonstration of the reaper in the year of Sitting Bull's birth and was widely marketing his invention within a few years. These agricultural implements did much to make westward expansion possible.[16]

Gold also attracted Easterners, especially after its discovery at Sutter's Mill in California's Sacramento Valley in 1848. By the next year, "forty-niners" were swarming into California, tens of thousands trekking across the Great Plains and mountains, the wealthy traveling by boat around Cape Horn. The trip had been made a little less daunting by the opening of the Oregon Trail in 1842. Gold prospectors, farmers, and others seeking a new life or following the call of manifest destiny—the belief that the United States was destined to rule the vast expanse of land from ocean to ocean, and from Canada south to the Rio Grande—set out with what they could haul in a wagon or pack on a mule. The Oregon Trail started in St. Louis, Missouri, and wound northwestward across the future states of Kansas, Nebraska, Wyoming, and Idaho to the northwest. Those heading to California could turn southwestward in Idaho and angle downward to the hoped-for land of riches.

There were other reasons for traveling west as well, including the desire of missionaries to bring Christianity and what they perceived as civilization to the Indians. Whatever the reason, travelers to the West crossed land that Sitting Bull and other tribal leaders saw as theirs.[17]

EARLY ENCOUNTERS WITH EUROAMERICANS

Sitting Bull initially was largely unaware of these historical forces at work. Through the first half of the 1850s, he had little contact with Wasichus, that is, Euroamericans, except for traders. Hunkpapas traded at Fort Pierre, previously part of the American Fur Company but by then operated by Pierre Chouteau and Company. Fort Pierre stood on the Missouri River near its conjunction with Bad River in Dakota Territory, a location now in South Dakota. Sitting Bull encountered traders both there and during their visits to his village. He knew well that the traders' people were responsible for forcing the buffalo herds farther west and spreading diseases such as smallpox, measles, and cholera among the Indians. Yet, as Thomas Jefferson had foreseen, the Hunkpapas, like other tribes, had grown dependent on manufactured goods available in trade. Guns and ammunition headed the list of desirable, increasingly necessary, items; but many other objects, including cooking utensils, tools, and containers, also proved popular as they replaced items that the Lakotas otherwise laboriously had to make. The primary currency for trading was the animal hide, especially buffalo hides and robes.

Sitting Bull's people also traded at Forts Berthold and Clark farther up the Missouri River in present-day North Dakota, and with the Slotas, also known as Métis, who were of mixed French and Indian descent. The Slotas, with whom the Lakotas alternately fought as well as traded, lived along the Red River of the North in Canada. They periodically brought trading goods, including guns and ammunition, south in two-wheeled carts.

Sitting Bull had mixed feelings about the white-skinned traders from the East, but he had no natural hatred toward Euroamericans. On the whole, he simply wanted them to leave his people alone. He and his Hunkpapas, as well as the larger Lakota community, saw other Indian tribes, such as the Crows, as their natural enemies and the source of honor in war. Only when it became obvious that Euroamerican incursions into Lakota territory endangered their way of life, as well as their very lives, did Sitting Bull come to view the intruders as enemies.

By the 1850s, Sitting Bull and tribes of the Great Plains in general were increasingly understanding this growing threat. The U.S. government by then was actively moving on several fronts to make westward expansion easier and safer. The government wanted to establish travel routes and, in the next decade, railroads. To make crossing the country less threatening, treaties sought to limit tribes to certain areas and to prevent intertribal warfare as well as conflict with travelers. At the same time, the government continued to construct military forts throughout Indian land.

Toward this end, the U.S. government proposed the Fort Laramie Treaty of 1851, which was designed to establish peace between tribes and the government, as well as among tribes, on the premise that even intertribal warfare might spill over and endanger travelers. The treaty authorized construction of forts and roads, established boundaries for individual tribes, and guaranteed protection for Indians from "the commission of all depredations by the people of the said United States." In addition, the government promised $50,000 annually for 50 years, a term later reduced to 10 years with the possibility of another five years "at the discretion of the President of the United States." Precisely how to make the annual payment—"in provisions, merchandise, domestic animals, and agricultural implements"—was also at the President's discretion. The treaty lists six Sioux signers but makes no distinctions among Lakota tribes. In any case, no Hunkpapas signed the treaty.[18] U.S. government representatives lacked the knowledge to make distinctions among Hunkpapa, Oglala, and other Sioux tribes, thus persisting in the belief that some chiefs could make commitments for all of the Lakota peoples and consequently lodging many mistaken claims of treaty-breaking.

BEGINNING OF THE PLAINS WARS

Sitting Bull was not involved with the Laramie Treaty of 1851; in fact, he may not have even been aware of it at the time. An incident occurred a few years later, however, that did touch Sitting Bull directly and make him acutely aware of the U.S. government and its soldiers. After the 1851 treaty, westward migration increased quickly. Approximately 60,000 people and 12,000 wagons, for example, passed by Fort Laramie in southeastern Wyoming during 1852. This heavy traffic created friction with the Indian tribes along the travelers' route.[19]

On August 18, 1854, a Mormon wagon train was heading toward Fort Laramie when a Brulé named High Forehead captured and butchered an ox that had wandered off from the train. Realizing that this act could cause trouble, the Brulé chief Brave Bear went to the fort and asked that everyone wait until the Indian agent returned so that he could help resolve the matter. Lieutenant John Grattan, believing that immediate action was necessary to control the Brulés, took 29 soldiers, an interpreter, and two cannons to their camp. Brave Bear offered to pay for the ox, but Grattan demanded that he surrender High Forehead. Tiring of the negotiations, Grattan ordered his men to open fire with rifles and cannons. Brave Bear was hit immediately and killed. In response, hundreds of Brulé warriors charged the soldiers and killed all of them in what government responses termed the Grattan Massacre. The incident was the opening volley in what came to be known as the Sioux Wars, or the Plains Wars.[20]

When Secretary of War Jefferson Davis, later president of the Confederacy, learned of the battle, he ordered Brigadier General William Harney to lead a campaign against the Sioux. Harney's forces arrived in the summer of 1855 and attacked a Brulé camp near Fort Laramie on September 3. The Brulés, under Little Thunder, successor to Brave Bear, were soundly defeated, with 86 killed and 70 women and children taken captive.[21] Harney then led his troops across Dakota to Fort Pierre, where in the spring of 1856 he summoned Lakota chiefs.

Sitting Bull's uncle, the Hunkpapa Four Horns, and his brother-in-law, the Miniconjou chief Makes Room, were among those present. Harney dictated terms to the chiefs: They must turn over any warriors who had killed whites, return all stolen property, and stay away from routes traveled by non-Indians. In return, they would receive protection and annuities. Harney also appointed a head chief for each tribe and made him accountable for the behavior of his people, naming Bear's Rib for the Hunkpapas. Harney permitted head chiefs to name subchiefs. Among those chosen for their respective groups were Four Horns and Makes Room. Sitting Bull certainly knew well what was occurring at Fort Pierre and, given his status as a war chief and closeness to Four Horns and Makes Room, probably was in attendance.[22]

Like most who spoke on behalf of the U.S. government, Harney knew little about the political and social workings of the tribes with which he came in contact. The tribes normally did not have one head chief, and no chief could by himself command absolute obedience. Decision making was collective and relied heavily on building consensus; in addition, given the importance of individual heroics as an avenue for proving oneself, chiefs could not completely control what individual warriors did. The heavy regimentation and demand for total obedience to orders endemic in the structure of the U.S. military were alien to the concept of warfare as waged by the Plains Indians.

Harney's directives therefore were doomed to failure. His quick resort to violence and authoritarian demeanor, though, surely were instructive for Sitting Bull, who was learning much about the men he would soon be fighting. When Harney left the region within a few months and the military abandoned Fort Pierre not long afterward, the so-called Harney Treaty for all practical purposes ceased to exist.

During the remainder of the decade, Sitting Bull and his Hunkpapas continued their battles with the Crows and other Indian enemies.[23] At the same time, they occasionally engaged Euroamericans when they passed too closely by Hunkpapa territory. Although direct attacks on forts were not common, an assault on Fort Union in northeastern Montana took place on August 11, 1860. Sitting Bull likely participated, although no definitive record places him there. About 250 Hunkpapas and Lakota Blackfeet attacked the fort. Initially, the soldiers inside withheld fire while the attackers killed cattle and burned wagons, firewood, and haystacks. When they tried to set fire to the fort, soldiers finally started shooting, and the Lakotas withdrew.

COMPROMISE OR CONFLICT?

At the beginning of the 1860s, two factions began to grow further apart within the Lakota community. Labeling them the peace and war factions would be too simplistic. One, led by Bear's Rib, sought accommodation with the U.S. government, believing that this approach was the only way to achieve peace, prevent great destruction to their people, and retain at least something of their old way of life. Sitting Bull would increasingly become the leader of the other faction, which saw the newcomers as a deadly threat to their own traditions and values. Sitting Bull sought peace with the U.S. government, but a peace that would preserve the Lakota culture. He saw the reservation culture as fundamentally incompatible with the Lakota way of life, and he would maintain that position as long as he had the capacity to do so.

In 1862, five events occurred that had major ramifications for Sitting Bull and the Hunkpapas: the execution of Bear's Rib, the discovery of gold in the Rocky Mountains, the Homestead Act, Congressional authorization for a transcontinental railroad, and the revolt in Minnesota of the Dakota division of the Sioux.

Lakotas were still receiving their annual annuities in 1862, but increasing numbers of Lakotas believed that to accept the goods was to compromise with the enemy. Bear's Rib announced that he would receive the items one final time, but that proved one time too many for him. On June 5, a group of Miniconjous and Sans Arcs arrived at the new Fort Pierre, built about two miles from the old one, and the site of the annuities dispersal. They announced that they had come to kill Bear's Rib. Bear's Rib heard of the threat and, perhaps driven by a sense of personal honor, arrived at the fort the next day. Two Sans Arcs, Mouse and One That Limps, approached Bear's Rib. Mouse shot him with his musket while Bear's Rib returned fire with his shotgun. Both men fell dead. Bear's Rib's men then killed One That Limps.

Sitting Bull had nothing to do with the killing, but the execution showed the growing dissatisfaction with the U.S. government and with those leaders who sought to coexist with its treaties and representatives. To Sitting Bull as well as to many others, the path of resistance called ever louder.

This path was reinforced by the discovery of gold in the Rocky Mountains, which greatly increased travel westward, especially along the Missouri River. The more Euroamericans that Sitting Bull saw, the greater seemed the threat. Those numbers were increased by passage of the Homestead Act of 1862, which offered 160 acres of public land to any homesteader who would live on and cultivate the land for five years while paying a fee of $18 to record ownership. Ultimately, 30 states would be opened to homesteading, including all those from the Midwest and westward, south to Texas, and north to Canada, until about 10 percent of U.S. land would be homesteaded.[24] Congress that same year authorized construction of a railroad that would connect East and West. The Central Pacific Railroad would build east from Sacramento, California, the Union Pacific west from Omaha, Nebraska. The railroads were given free land through what, of course, was Indian country, as well as sizable loans. Although the specific railroad that Sitting Bull would face was the Northern Pacific rather than this transcontinental railroad, the Congressional action taken in 1862 made railroad building a matter of national pride and guaranteed that it would have strong support regardless of Indian concerns. Not until after the conclusion of the Civil War, however, would money be available for extensive railroad construction; at that point they began to present, in Sitting Bull's eyes, yet another threat to his people.

Meanwhile, farther east, the Dakota Sioux were chafing at a number of injustices. Much of their land had been taken, and money that should have gone to the Dakotas instead was paid directly to fur traders, supposedly to settle debts owed by the Dakotas. Further, promised food rations often were late or reduced in violation of treaties signed in 1837. Finally, resentment boiled over, and parties of Dakotas in the summer of 1862 attacked settlers living near their reservation on the Minnesota River. About 600 settlers were killed and 300 captured before the uprising was put down. In the aftermath, the remaining Dakota land was confiscated. The Dakotas were moved to a reservation in South Dakota, imprisoned (38 of whom were hanged the day after Christmas, 1862, in the largest mass execution in U.S. history), or fled westward. Inkpaduta, a Dakota chief who had led an earlier and bloody uprising in 1857, was among those who fled toward Lakota land. The Dakota experience in Minnesota further inflamed the situation in the Great Plains, and Inkpaduta became an ally of Sitting Bull during the conflicts of the 1860s and 1870s.[25]

BATTLE OF KILLDEER MOUNTAIN

Pursuing Dakota refugees, General Henry Sibley, who had served as Minnesota's first governor after statehood was achieved in 1858, led an army from Minnesota into Dakota Territory. General Alfred Sully led another army up the Missouri River. The army's July 1863 encounters with the Lakota Hunkpapas and Blackfeet, who had been joined by a large contingent of Dakotas, at the Battles of Dead Buffalo Lake and Stony Lake in present-day North Dakota signaled the beginning of open warfare between Sitting Bull's Hunkpapas and the U.S. military. Both battles were victories for the army, whose cavalry and artillery forced their adversaries to retreat westward. Sitting Bull apparently participated in these battles. Pictograph 24 in Sitting Bull's first pictographic autobiography depicts him striking a soldier with a coup stick and capturing a mule, actions believed to have occurred at Dead Buffalo Lake.[26]

Almost exactly one year later, on July 28, 1864, Sitting Bull was involved in another battle with General Sully's troops. The site of the conflict was

Killdeer Mountain in northwestern North Dakota. One of General Sully's soldiers rode too far in advance of the rest of the troops and was ambushed and killed by three Dakota warriors. Cavalry arrived quickly and shot the three Dakotas, after which one of the soldiers cut off their heads. General Sully ordered the heads to be hanged on a hill as a visible warning against further transgressions. Outraged by this incident, the Sioux gathered about 3,000 warriors. The large assemblage included Sitting Bull, his uncle Chief Four Horns, and his nephew White Bull, who at age 14 was preparing for his first battle against U.S. government forces.

On July 28, Sully's army of approximately 2,200 approached the Sioux camp near the base of Killdeer Mountain. The Sioux, including Lakotas, Dakotas under Inkpaduta, and Yanktonais, went out to meet the army, but the army's fire power—rifles and cannons versus the Indians' muskets and bows and arrows—was too strong for them. The Sioux steadily fell back toward their village.

Although large armies may share the field of battle, the battle itself is often an amalgamation of many individual actions. That was especially true for the Sioux, who so highly valued personal glory and honor. One of the most remarkable individual efforts at Killdeer Mountain involved a Hunkpapa who had been crippled all his life and unable to walk. He resolved to make a contribution to the battle, although he knew that he would likely die in the attempt. Bear's Heart, also known as Man Who Never Walked, had himself strapped into a travois pulled by a horse. The horse was lashed until it started running toward the army. Gunfire quickly ended the lives of both the horse and the man, but Man Who Never Walked died a warrior's death. Among those wounded during the battle was Four Horns, who was shot in the back. Sitting Bull and White Bull rushed to his rescue, and Sitting Bull tended to his wound, thus missing the final portion of the battle as the soldiers overran the village.

The Sioux began their retreat, taking what they could with them, but advancing soldiers destroyed most of their provisions and tipis. Perhaps 100 Sioux died in the Battle of Killdeer Mountain; Sully's forces lost only two men. Sully was most directly after Dakotas who had fled Minnesota after the 1862 uprising. Although he ended up attacking a much wider grouping of Sioux, he nonetheless achieved a portion of his objective, as many of the dead were indeed Minnesota Dakotas. Inkpaduta survived and led the remaining members of his group farther east, departing from Sitting Bull and the rest of the Sioux.

This was Sitting Bull's first major battle with a large government force and despite the defeat, he was not ready to give up. During the next week, his Hunkpapas were joined by additional Miniconjous, Sans Arcs, and

Brulés, as well as Cheyenne warriors. From August 7 to August 9, they tried to take advantage of the rugged terrain of the Badlands near Heart River in North Dakota by harassing the army's advance or rear guard and killing livestock. Artillery, however, kept them from closing in and doing much damage. With the attackers' casualties mounting and little in the way of supplies, Sitting Bull wisely urged withdrawal.[27]

CAPTAIN FISK AND FANNY KELLY

The next battle with Euroamericans would leave Sitting Bull wounded. Near the end of August, Sitting Bull's Hunkpapas spotted a train of about 100 wagons commanded by Captain James L. Fisk, who was taking people to the mines. Fifty soldiers escorted the party. For several days, the Hunkpapas observed and waited for an advantageous moment to attack without taking on the entire body of travelers.

On September 2, a wagon broke down, and about a dozen men, most of them soldiers, stopped to make the repairs. Sitting Bull led approximately 100 warriors toward the wagon. According to Utley, it was at this time that Sitting Bull was wounded. Because there was more honor in physically touching and struggling with an enemy than killing him from a distance, Sitting Bull rode up to a mounted soldier and started to struggle with him, trying to throw the soldier to the ground. The soldier, whose military training included nothing about counting coup but much about winning as efficiently as possible, pulled his pistol and shot Sitting Bull in the left hip, the bullet coming out his back. Jumping Bull, Sitting Bull's adopted brother, and White Bull reached their wounded war chief and led him to safety. Jumping Bull, who had learned some basic medicine, managed to stop the bleeding and bandaged Sitting Bull.

The remaining group of men who had stopped with the wagon were killed or wounded, and the Hunkpapas withdrew after additional soldiers arrived from the wagon train. The miners and soldiers then formed a simple fort by circling their wagons and piling sod against them. They named this rudimentary fort Fort Dilts after Jefferson Dilts, one of the men killed in the recent fight. The conflict, much smaller in scope than the encounters with General Sully, and fought more in line with traditional Lakota hit-and-run tactics, was more successful for the Hunkpapas than the earlier battles despite the wound to Sitting Bull.[28]

Stanley Vestal gives a different account of Sitting Bull's wounding. According to Vestal, after the group had established its fortifications, word of their difficulty came to General Sully, who ordered a contingent of 600 soldiers to their rescue. When they arrived, fighting ensued, and Sitting

Bull charged a soldier who was on foot. The soldier shot Sitting Bull and then mounted his horse and rode off.[29] Sitting Bull's pictograph 13 gives yet a third version. In Sitting Bull's own rendition, the soldier is on foot but has already been hit in the back by an arrow that is protruding out his chest. Despite his serious wound, the soldier shoots Sitting Bull. These different versions are easy to understand when one realizes that historians writing about the Plains Indians are working with few relevant written documents because most Indians did not write. Vestal had recourse to eyewitnesses, but they were recalling events from long ago and from their own individual perspectives.

Among the more interesting episodes from Sitting Bull's life at this time was his encounter with a white woman named Fanny Kelly. She, her husband, and their niece and adopted daughter, Mary J. Hurley, seven or eight years old, were members of a small party migrating from Kansas to Idaho in July 1864 when they were attacked by an Oglala war party that killed three of the men. Mr. Kelly escaped, two other men were wounded but survived, and Fanny and Mary, along with another woman and her son, were taken captive. Fanny helped Mary escape, but the child was later killed. During five months in captivity, Fanny Kelly was forced to travel and live with the Oglalas, then traded to the Hunkpapa, Brings Plenty, who made her his wife. She was with the Lakotas during the battle of Killdeer Mountain and the attack on Captain Fisk's wagon train.

Several offers to purchase Kelly's freedom were made by emissaries from her husband, but Brings Plenty resolutely refused all offers until Sitting Bull, with his friend Crawler, summoned the reluctant trader to his tipi and compelled him at gunpoint to yield the woman. Fanny, who had been named Real Woman in recognition of her hard work and efforts to please her captors (both survival tactics), stayed with Crawler and his wife until she could be escorted to Fort Sully, above Fort Pierre on the Missouri. White Bull remembered his uncle expressing sincere sympathy for Fanny Kelly's predicament and her homesickness. Although Sitting Bull was primarily responsible for her freedom, she did not acknowledge her debt to him in her memoir, which was published in 1871.[30]

EXPANSION OF THE WAR

During the mid-1860s, a number of events occurred that did not directly involve Sitting Bull but that hardened his determination to resist the U.S. soldiers, because they either intensified Sitting Bull's suspicions regarding the soldiers or encouraged him to believe that they could be defeated. In November 1864, at Sand Creek, Colorado, militia under Colonel John M. Chivington attacked a camp of southern Cheyennes led by

Chief Black Kettle, who had remained peaceful and friendly to the U.S. government. Arapahos also were in the village. Chivington's forces killed approximately 150 Cheyennes and Arapahos, mainly women, children, and the elderly, in what even the famous scout Kit Carson labeled a massacre.[31]

The Fetterman battle, or massacre, depending on one's point of view, took place in late December 1866 near Fort Phil Kearney in north-central Wyoming. Here the outcome would be quite different from what transpired at Sand Creek. With the forts proving a growing irritant to the Plains Indians, a large force of Lakotas (mainly Miniconjous and Oglalas) and Cheyennes developed a plan to lead soldiers away from the fort and ambush them. The great Oglala chief Red Cloud is often credited with overall leadership of the resistance to Fort Phil Kearney and other forts in the area, although his specific role in this battle remains uncertain. When a wood train left the fort to cut wood, Crazy Horse, a revered Oglala warrior, led an attack on it. A relief effort was hurriedly formed under Captain William J. Fetterman, who was directed by his commanding officer, Colonel Henry Carrington, not to pursue Indians beyond Lodge Trail Ridge because the soldiers could not see what might be on the other side. Fetterman, who had boasted that with 80 men he could ride through the entire Sioux nation, ironically led a force of 80 men out of Fort Phil Kearney that day.

Once Fetterman approached the attacking Indians, Crazy Horse led his men in a zigzag pattern away from the fort and toward the forbidden ridge. Fetterman, ignoring his orders, led his men in pursuit. Once beyond the ridge and out of sight of the fort, he was attacked by the waiting Indians. Fetterman and all of his men were killed in what the Lakotas referred to as the Battle of One Hundred White Men Killed—the worst U.S. military defeat in the Indian wars until Little Bighorn 10 years later.[32]

A subsequent battle did not go so well for Red Cloud. He attempted a similar approach in July 1867 in the Wagon Box Fight. Crazy Horse again led the decoy party, attacking a group of woodcutters outside Fort Phil Kearney. This time, however, the attacked men had new breech-loading Springfield rifles that could fire rapidly. The heavy rain of bullets, which the attackers had never experienced before, kept them at bay and short-circuited their plans.[33]

The conflicts between Plains tribes and U.S. government forces continued while at the same time the government pursued new peace treaties. In 1865, General Sully issued invitations to come to Fort Rice, located near the confluence of the Cannonball and Missouri Rivers in North Dakota, for discussions. By July, a large village of Hunkpapa, Blackfeet, and Yanktonai tipis was set up near the fort. In the camp was Sitting Bull, the Strong Heart war chief, who remained highly skeptical of the peace effort and argued strongly against acceding to Sully's invitation. The majority opinion, however, was to seek a truce. As General Sully and his army approached the fort, an inexperienced colonel decided to honor him with a salute and ordered his artillery to fire.[34]

The sudden discharge shocked the surrounding Sioux, who imagined another Sand Creek Massacre. Many fled, and rumors quickly spread. Sitting Bull, returning from a hunting expedition, met a villager fleeing on horseback who said that General Sully had killed all those who had entered the fort to smoke the pipe with him. Sitting Bull immediately rode through the villages urging everyone to leave immediately. Most did so, ending Sully's peace effort. Whether Sitting Bull genuinely feared an attack by the soldiers or seized the opportunity to push his position against compromising with the army is impossible to know for sure. In either case, he undoubtedly acted in what he considered his people's best interests.

Sitting Bull then gathered about 300 warriors and, on July 28, 1865, attacked Fort Rice. Painted red and riding his favorite war horse, Bloated Jaw, Sitting Bull led the initial charge. The attack was not successful against the heavily guarded fort, although Sitting Bull captured two horses. Capturing the enemy's horses was always a source of honor among the Lakotas. Utley references an army newspaper, *Frontier Scout*, in which Sitting Bull's warriors are angry with Sitting Bull for apparently settling for the horses and not continuing the fight, but it is important to recognize that the source can hardly be considered authoritative or impartial.[35]

An August 8 report by General Sully includes the first written reference to Sitting Bull in English, although he enjoyed great renown among the Lakotas and other tribes. Sully wrote that "a chief (who wishes to lead the war party) called Sitting Bull . . . went through the different villages cutting himself with a knife" while warning the villagers of the killings that had been erroneously reported to him. Sitting Bull's nephew One Bull denied that he had cut himself but otherwise confirmed Sully's account. Self-mutilation, however, as in the Sun Dance, was a respected way for a leader to affirm his commitment to his people. Giving one's flesh was an offering to Wakantanka that he might protect his people. Before the Battle of the Rosebud in 1876, for example, Sitting Bull had Jumping Bear remove 50 pieces of flesh from each of Sitting Bull's arms with an awl.[36]

After this incident, Sitting Bull's Hunkpapas headed west toward Powder River in southeastern Montana. There they encountered two of General Patrick Edward Connor's columns under the leadership of Colonel Nelson Cole and Lieutenant Colonel Samuel Walker. On September 5, 1865, carrying the shield that his father had given him many years before, Sitting Bull led a group of warriors attacking from the east. White Bull later stated that Sitting Bull did not distinguish himself in that battle, perhaps because, as Utley argues, he had been listening closely to his mother's warnings that he needed to think about his family and what would happen to them if he were killed.[37] Yet Sitting Bull could not have seen the engagement as a terrible embarrassment, for he included the battle in his first pictographic autobiography—in drawing number 27.

The Lakota hit-and-run tactics did not inflict heavy casualties, but they took their toll on the soldiers' stamina and morale. After Sitting Bull and his warriors withdrew, the weather turned surprisingly cold. A large number of the army's horses, short on feed and water, died, forcing Cole and Walker to abandon much of their supplies and lead their tired, discouraged troops, many of them on foot, back to their base at Camp Connor, later Fort Reno, on the Powder River.[38]

In the fall of 1865, a government peace commission concluded a series of treaties with representatives from all of the Lakota tribes, as well as the Yanktonais, although the representatives generally came from those elements within the tribes that were willing to compromise with the government and live on reservations. A great many Lakotas were not willing to do that, especially among the Hunkpapas and Oglalas. The treaty with the Hunkpapas, concluded in October and ratified the next spring, on March 17, 1866, included provisions similar to those in the Fort Laramie Treaty of 1851, except for the financial terms. The treaty promised each lodge or family $30 annually for 20 years. Sitting Bull, of course, neither participated in the peace discussions nor signed the treaty.[39]

While the treaty was being ratified, Sitting Bull was attacking Fort Rice. When Fort Buford was constructed later that summer in northwestern North Dakota, Sitting Bull turned his attention to it as the fort marked an even further intrusion of government soldiers into Hunkpapa territory. Two days before Christmas, in an especially insulting gesture, Sitting Bull seized the fort's sawmill and icehouse on the Missouri riverbank. Artillery fire forced him to abandon the position, but he returned the next morning, singing loudly and beating time on the circular saw until soldiers from the fort attacked the sawmill and Sitting Bull and his men withdrew.

Other forts also came in for harassment by Sitting Bull, including Fort Union to the west of Fort Buford in Montana, and Fort Stevenson to its east. As 1866 yielded to 1867, Sitting Bull had not the slightest inclination to negotiate any agreement with his enemy, consistently demanding that the soldiers, miners, buffalo hunters, and other unwelcome visitors pull out of his land and leave his people, as well as the buffalo and woodlands, alone. The buffalo were essentially the lifeblood of the Lakotas, but Sitting Bull also resented losing trees to the intruders, who chopped them down for forts, homes, and firewood. Those were his terms for peace, but they were terms the U.S. government was decidedly not going to accept.

NOTES

1. Robert M. Utley, *The Lance and the Shield: The Life and Times of Sitting Bull* (1993; New York: Ballantine Books, 1994), 32–33.

2. The Little Wound's explanation is translated by Antoine Herman and published in James R. Walker's *Lakota Belief and Ritual*, ed. Raymond J. DeMallie and Elaine A. Jahner (1980; Lincoln: University of Nebraska Press, 1991), 69.

3. Walker, 103, 120.

4. Walker, 156.

5. Utley, 29.

6. Utley, 30.

7. Stanley Vestal, *Warpath: The True Story of the Fighting Sioux Told in a Biography of Chief White Bull* (1934; Lincoln: University of Nebraska Press, 1984), 201; Utley, 57.

8. Utley, 28.

9. Sitting Bull's first pictographic autobiography is known as *The Kimball Pictographic Record* after the physician, Dr. James Kimball, who acquired a copy of the original drawings in 1870. The series is published in *Three Pictographic Autobiographies of Sitting Bull*, edited by M. W. Stirling (Washington, DC: Smithsonian Institution, 1938). See pictographic illustrations 28, 29, 30, and 32.

10. Utley, 129–30.

11. Vestal, *Warpath*, 140; Utley, 58–59.

12. Utley, 101; Stanley Vestal, *Sitting Bull: Champion of the Sioux,* 2nd ed. (1957; Norman: University of Oklahoma Press, 1989), 96; Vestal, *New Sources of Indian History 1850–1891* (Norman, University of Oklahoma Press, 1934), 231–33.

13. Utley, 25.

14. Utley, 40, 42.

15. Donald Jackson, ed. *Letters of the Lewis and Clark Expedition with Related Documents 1783–1854* (Urbana: University of Illinois Press, 1962), 11.

16. For studies of the impact of Deere and McCormick, see Neil Dahlstrom, *The John Deere Story: A Biography of Plowmakers John & Charles Deere* (DeKalb: Northern Illinois University Press, 2005); and Cyrus McCormick, *The Century of the Reaper: An Account of Cyrus Hall McCormick, the Inventor of the Reaper* (Boston: Houghton Mifflin, 1931).

17. For further information about the historical forces just outlined, see Alexander B. Adams, *Sitting Bull: An Epic of the Plains* (New York: G. P. Putnam's Sons, 1973), 19–30.

18. Charles J. Kappler, ed. *Indian Affairs: Laws and Treaties,* 7 vols. (1904–41; Washington, DC: U.S. Government Printing Office, 1975–79), 2: 594–96.

19. Charles M. Robinson III, *The Plains Wars 1757–1900* (Osceola, WI: Osprey, 2003), 32.

20. Robinson, 32. Brave Bear is referred to as Conquering Bear in Utley, 45.

21. Robinson, 35.

22. Utley, 46.

23. See the battles with Indian tribes discussed in Chapter 2.

24. For a succinct examination of the Homestead Act, see Paul Wallace Gates, *Free*

Homesteads for All Americans: The Homestead Act of 1862 (Washington, DC: Civil War Centennial Commission, 1962).

25. Michael Clodfelter presents a careful analysis of the Dakota uprising in his *The Dakota War: The United States Army versus the Sioux, 1862–1865* (Jefferson, NC: McFarland, 1998). A recent discussion of the earlier 1857 Dakota uprising occurs in Susan J. Michno's "The Spirit Lake Massacre: Death and Captivity," *Wild West*, February 2006, 46–52. President Abraham Lincoln's involvement in saving most of the condemned Dakotas from hanging is detailed in Hank H. Cox, *Lincoln and the Sioux Uprising of 1862* (Nashville: Cumberland House, 2005). A contemporary and sympathetic account of the Dakotas' rebellion is given by Sarah F. Wakefield in her *Six Weeks in the Sioux Tepees* (1863; Guilford, CT: Globe Pequot, 2004). The book is an account of her time spent as a captive of the Dakotas. The second edition of Wakefield's captivity narrative is available in *Women's Indian Captivity Narratives*, ed. Kathryn Zabelle Derounian-Stodola (New York: Penguin Books, 1998), 235–313.

26. Vestal's identification of the content of pictograph 24 occurs on page 19 of this edition.

27. Vestal, *Sitting Bull*, 53–57; Utley, 54–58.

28. Utley, 59–60.

29. Vestal, *Sitting Bull*, 63.

30. Vestal, Sitting Bull, 64–68; Utley, 60, 63; Fanny Kelly, *Narrative of My Captivity among the Sioux Indians* (Cincinnati: Wilstach, Baldwin & Co., 1871). A modern edition of Kelly's memoir is available and is edited by Clark and Mary Lee Spence in the Legends of the West series (Old Saybrook, CT: Konecky and Konecky, 1990). In addition to ignoring Sitting Bull, Kelly withholds the fact that she was taken as a wife by Brings Plenty. Her omissions and distortions result from her desire to place herself in the best possible light given her contemporaries' attitudes toward Indians. Brings Plenty did not seem to bear a lasting grudge against Sitting Bull for depriving him of Kelly. Much later, apparently during the Ghost Dance phenomenon of 1890, Brings Plenty sent a note to Sitting Bull urging him to come to Pine Ridge Agency. Although the note is somewhat unclear, it appears to request Sitting Bull's involvement in the overthrow of the Euroamericans supposedly promised by the dance. Brings Plenty signs his note with the common but nonetheless quite friendly statement, "I shake hands with you all." See Vestal, *New Sources*, 39–40.

31. See Dee Brown, *The American West* (1994; New York: Simon and Schuster, 1995), 100–09; Larry McMurtry, *Oh What a Slaughter: Massacres in the American West* (New York: Simon and Schuster, 2005), 91–113; and the Web site for the National Parks Service Northern Cheyenne Sand Creek Massacre Project (<http:www.sandcreek.org>). An interesting fictional exploration of the Sand Creek Massacre from a twentieth-century perspective appears in Margaret Coel's *The Story Teller* (1998; New York: Penguin, 1999).

32. Brown, 90–96; Vestal, *Warpath*, 50–69. White Bull claimed that Red Cloud was not present at the Fetterman battle and argued to Vestal that the Oglala chief was given credit for several battles that he did not lead. Frank Grouard, who lived for a time with Sitting Bull and will be discussed in the next chapter, claimed that Red Cloud did not have a high regard for Sitting Bull [Joe DeBarthe, *Life and Adventures of Frank Grouard*, ed. Edgar I. Stewart (Norman: University of Oklahoma Press, 1958), 250]. White Bull may be taking the side of his uncle in denigrating Red Cloud's accomplishments. If so, Vestal, who grew so close to Sitting Bull's nephew that the by-then elderly chief adopted Vestal as a son and named him Ocastonka, which means "famous," likely would have accepted a pro-Sitting Bull position. See Raymond J. DeMallie's Foreword to *Warpath*, xi. For a balanced consideration of Red Cloud's possible role in the Fetterman Massacre, see Robert W. Larson,

Red Cloud: Warrior-Statesman of the Lakota Sioux (Norman: University of Oklahoma Press, 1997), 99–100.

33. Brown, 96–98; Vestal, *Warpath,* 70–83.

34. Vestal, *Sitting Bull,* 70–74; Utley, 67–68.

35. Utley, 68; 466–47, notes 2 and 6.

36. Utley, 67–68; 346, n. 4; 137–38.

37. Utley, 69–70.

38. Vestal, *Sitting Bull,* 80.

39. The terms of the Hunkpapa treaty are printed in Kappler, 2: 901–03. The edition reverses the signatures between the Hunkpapa and Yanktonai treaties; for the correct Hunkpapa signatures, see 2: 904.

Chapter 4

FAILED PEACE EFFORTS
(1867–1873)

FATHER DE SMET'S PEACE MISSION

The American Civil War ended in 1865, but the cessation of the war between the North and South promised no respite for the Indians of the Plains. Their lot would become worse, for ending the war that pitted brother against brother opened the door for greater resources to be put into the simmering conflict that few Euroamericans saw as being waged against equals, let alone brothers. The general attitude toward Indians was that they were human but clearly inferior—uncivilized savages, non-Christians needing conversion to make them more thoroughly human. At best they were seen as childlike beings requiring adults (that is, those of lighter skin) to teach them how to think, dress, work, and act—in short, how to live. The Indian must be remade in the Euroamerican's image because, after all, it was the latter who was made in God's image. Or so the vast majority believed. And with the end of the Civil War, more money and human resources could be directed toward that transformation, which at the same time would open up more farming land, timber, gold deposits, waterways, and railroad routes.

There were, of course, exceptions to these attitudes, even among those who hoped to win converts to Christianity—some who respected, even loved Indians and did indeed see them as brothers and sisters. Father Peter John De Smet, a Jesuit Roman Catholic priest, was one of those exceptions. Committed to both peace and the Indians with whom he had worked since 1838, and convinced that war for the Indians meant extinction, Father De Smet set out on April 21, 1868, on the first leg of his effort to persuade Sitting Bull and the other "hostile" Indians to agree to discuss peace at Fort Laramie.

This effort followed the Medicine Lodge treaties of the previous year with the southern Plains tribes at Medicine Lodge, Kansas.[1] Now the attention of the Indian Peace Commission, established by the U.S. Congress on July 20, 1867, turned to the northern Plains tribes. The peace commissioners arrived at Fort Laramie on November 9, hoping that Red Cloud of the Oglalas, whom the U.S. government viewed as the most important Indian chief among the Sioux, would be present. Red Cloud, however, was not there, having made his position clear: no peace agreement without removal of the forts along the Bozeman Trail, which stretched from Julesburg, Colorado, to the goldfields in Montana, running past Fort Laramie and continuing beyond the Powder and Yellowstone Rivers. Named for John M. Bozeman, who had mapped the trail in the 1860s, the route was protected by Forts C. F. Smith, Phil Kearney, and Reno.

Ulysses S. Grant, as General of the Army of the United States, the military's commanding officer, decided to accept Red Cloud's condition and ordered the forts closed, although the Oglala chief refused to sign a treaty until the forts were actually abandoned. The closing began on July 29 with the army's departure from Fort C. F. Smith. Fort Phil Kearney closed a few days later. No sooner were the soldiers out than the Oglalas set the forts on fire. The closure of the forts was a huge political victory for Red Cloud, and he signed the Fort Laramie Treaty in November.[2]

Sitting Bull proved much less willing to enter into dialogue with the Peace Commission, hence Father De Smet's peace journey. It took the *Columbia*, departing Omaha on April 21, 1868, with De Smet aboard, 33 days to reach Fort Rice on the Missouri River as the captain contended with sandbars, snags, and uncertain currents. Along the way, Father De Smet conducted daily religious services in a room provided for his use as a chapel.[3]

At Fort Rice, De Smet greeted Indian leaders and awaited the peace commissioners, the first of whom, General Alfred H. Terry, arrived at the fort on May 31. De Smet received a warm welcome from the Indians at the fort and held councils with several tribes, meeting Hunkpapa representatives on May 25. In a progress report to Commissioner Nathaniel G. Taylor on May 30, De Smet wrote that the Indians at Fort Rice were worried about his safety, relaying that they "expressed a sincere anxiety of my proceeding to the hostile bands, in the Interior of their country & promised to give me a powerful escort to assist me in my endeavours." In that same report, he noted that a rider from "the hostile bands" had arrived saying that De Smet was expected and would be listened to.[4]

De Smet was far less worried about his safety than were the Indians at Fort Rice. Perhaps no non-Indian was so respected by a wide range of tribes over much of the continent as the Jesuit priest who had been journeying to serve, as he saw them, the spiritual and temporal needs of the tribes since 1838. Born in 1801 in Belgium, Pierre Jean De Smet emigrated to the United States in 1821 with several other young men aspiring to become Jesuit priests and missionaries to the American Indians. De Smet was ordained a priest in 1827 and became a citizen of the United States in 1833, at which time he formally changed his name to Peter John De Smet, symbolizing his acceptance of his new American identity.[5] Since then he had worked tirelessly on behalf of the Indians and made several trips to Europe to raise money for his missionary work.

When Father De Smet set out on the long overland journey to visit Sitting Bull, the Hunkpapa chief knew much about the man Indians often referred to as the "Black Robe" because of his clothing. He was one of the few Euroamericans that Sitting Bull trusted and respected, despite Sitting Bull's skepticism regarding Christianity, which he saw as a force generally allied with the U.S. government against his people.[6]

In early June, Father De Smet began his 300-mile journey to Sitting Bull's camp at the meeting of the Yellowstone and Powder Rivers in Montana. A party of about 80 Lakotas and Yanktonais accompanied De Smet on his "peace ride" to honor his effort and provide security, including such chiefs as the Hunkpapas Running Antelope and the younger Bear's Rib and the Yanktonai Two Bears. Blue Thunder, a Yanktonai who had scouted against the "hostile" Lakotas, drove De Smet's carriage—not a particularly wise choice for a driver. From a practical standpoint, the two most important members of the group were Charles Galpin, a trader much respected by Sitting Bull's Hunkpapas, and Galpin's wife, Matilda, also known as Eagle Woman, who was the daughter of a Hunkpapa-Two Kettle couple. Eagle Woman had chosen 10 women among the 80 escorts to show that the group came in peace. The Galpins were to act as interpreters, with Charles Galpin taking down in summary fashion what was said during meetings between De Smet and the Hunkpapas.

When Sitting Bull learned that Black Robe's party was on its way, he sent a delegation of 18 men to accompany and protect the visitor. On June 19, Father De Smet neared the camp, to be greeted by Sitting Bull and 400 warriors dressed in their best and singing in greeting. The most prestigious of the Hunkpapas joined Sitting Bull in this extraordinary reception, including Four Horns and Gall. Unfurled on the priest's carriage was a large banner, De Smet's "standard of peace," depicting the Virgin Mary surrounded by stars on one side of the banner and the name of Jesus printed on the other. The Virgin Mary was a reassuring and popular image for the Hunkpa-pas, who related to her as someone similar to White Buffalo Woman.

Not everyone in the Hunkpapa camp, though, welcomed De Smet. Some, such as White Gut, one of the war chiefs, wanted to kill both the priest and Blue Thunder. Knowing this, and determined to protect De Smet because he was both a guest and an esteemed friend, Sitting Bull took every precaution to ensure his visitor's safety and the safety of his party. The Black Robe and the Galpins stayed with Sitting Bull in his own lodge, guarded by Sitting Bull's most able and trusted akicita warriors. Other warriors guarded the party's horses.

That night, Sitting Bull assured Father De Smet, according to Galpin's note-taking, later written out more fully by De Smet, "I will listen to thy good words, and as bad as I have been to the whites, just so good am I ready to become toward them."[7] Sitting Bull's position was really no different from what it had been. If the Euroamericans left and abided by earlier treaties, there would be no trouble. In that case, Sitting Bull would indeed be "good" to them; unlike the Crows, for example, they were not his natural, traditional enemies. Sitting Bull fought them because he perceived a need to do so, not because he wanted to fight them or felt any cultural necessity to do so.

The next day, June 20, a large council lodge was constructed of 10 tipis. Four buffalo robes were placed as seats in the center of the lodge, and Father De Smet was escorted by several chiefs to one of them. Charles Galpin sat beside him, with Sitting Bull's uncle Four Horns, cousin Black Moon, and several other leaders, including, of course, Sitting Bull, also in the center. The crowd was immense, perhaps numbering 5,000, probably including many from other Lakota tribes, who gathered to hear what the Black Robe had to say.

Four Horns lit a peace pipe, extended it to Wakantanka and the four directions, and passed it to the most prominent individuals at the council, starting with Father De Smet. Black Moon then invited the guest to speak. De Smet spoke with great conviction, urging his listeners to stop fighting and meet with the commissioners at Fort Rice. He then had the Holy Virgin banner set up in the lodge and said that he would leave it as a sign of his commitment to the welfare of the Sioux.

Black Moon gave an answering address, expressing respect for De Smet's message but also citing a range of Euroamerican injustices, including establishing forts, slaughtering buffalo, cutting timber, and, of course, killing Indians. Sitting Bull then spoke. He announced that Hunkpapa representatives would return with Father De Smet to Fort Rice to meet with the commissioners and reiterated his desire to be a friend to his current enemies.

After finishing, Sitting Bull shook hands with Father De Smet, Charles Galpin, and Eagle Woman. As soon as Sitting Bull sat down, however, he jumped back up to say that he had forgotten certain points he wanted to make. He asserted that he would not sell any portion of his land and repeated some of his enduring conditions for peace: abandonment of forts and an end to cutting of timber along the Missouri River. These final comments elicited great applause from his audience.

Two Bears followed with a statement urging peace, and Running Antelope closed the council. Father De Smet was pleased with the results, looking forward optimistically to the negotiations at Fort Rice. He baptized a number of Indians and recounted stories from the Bible. Reports that he baptized Sitting Bull were false, but he did give the Hunkpapa chief a crucifix made of brass and wood that Sitting Bull valued highly. One of the best known portraits of Sitting Bull, taken by D. F. Barry around 1885, shows him wearing this crucifix around his neck, although there is some chance that he may be wearing a later gift from another priest, Father Francis Craft.

The council had been an extraordinary event, bringing together two of the greatest spiritual leaders of nineteenth-century America, the revered Wichasha Wakan, Sitting Bull, and a brave and dedicated Jesuit, Father De Smet. The two men genuinely respected and liked each other, but their respective aspirations for peace, noble but essentially incompatible within that historical moment, were doomed to failure.

FORT LARAMIE TREATY

After saying Mass early in the morning of June 21, Father De Smet started his return journey to Fort Rice, accompanied by a group of lesser chiefs, including Gall and Bull Owl. Sitting Bull and a group of akicita rode along as far as Powder River, both to protect and honor the Black Robe. Sitting Bull then shook hands with De Smet, reaffirmed his comments of the previous day, and returned to his village. He had instructed Gall to accept no presents, listen to the commissioners, and tell them that they must remove the soldiers and stop the steamboats from coming up the rivers.[8] Sitting Bull had promised to accept the decisions made by Gall and the rest of the contingent in council, but he clearly expected any agreement to include his often stated requirements, which he considered non-negotiable.

Gall told the commissioners (Generals Terry, William S. Harney, and John B. Sanborn, the last a former military figure who had served in the volunteer forces during the Civil War) what his people expected them to do. Then he signed the Fort Laramie Treaty by making his mark by, according to the common expression, "touching the pen." On the treaty Gall is noted by another name of his, The Man that Goes in the Middle. The treaty established the Great Sioux Reservation in the Dakota Territory west of the Missouri River. It identified the land north of the North Platte River and east of the Bighorn Mountains (roughly eastern Wyoming) as "unceded Indian territory" open to the Sioux for hunting as long as enough buffalo still roamed there "in such numbers as to justify the chase." The treaty promised that "no white person or persons" would be permitted to enter the area without permission of the Sioux. The provision so important to Red Cloud was included, declaring that the forts along the Bozeman Trail would be vacated. A provision that later would prove troublesome to the government stipulated that no reservation land could be taken without approval of "three-fourths of all adult male Indians occupying or interested in the same." The Indians, in exchange, would cease warfare and maintain peace.[9]

The Fort Laramie Treaty did not meet Sitting Bull's requirements, yet Gall signed it on July 2, seemingly doing an about-face after previously stating his position. Most likely, Gall, unable to read the treaty, assumed that it included what he had said it was to include and did not understand that the treaty had been completely drafted before his statement. Celebrations took place over the next two days, including a feast. Father De Smet, believing that a genuine peace had been achieved, experienced another cause for joy when, at Eagle Woman's request, he baptized her. He gave her the baptismal name of Matilda and then happily blessed the Galpins' marriage.[10]

RETURN TO WAR

The Fort Laramie Treaty offered Sitting Bull several options: become a reservation Indian, try to compromise with the Euroamericans while retaining as much of the old way of life as possible (perhaps by alternating between life on the reservation and hunting buffalo in the unceded territory), or hold fast to Lakota traditions and culture. Sitting Bull chose the third option.

If Sitting Bull needed additional evidence that the government representatives proposing treaties could not be trusted, he received it in November 1868 when soldiers again attacked Black Kettle of the Cheyenne. This time, the assault was led by Colonel George Armstrong Custer, known as Long Hair because of his long, flowing golden hair, who, to the sounds of his favorite song, "Garry Owen," led his troopers against Black Kettle's village on the Washita River in Oklahoma. This time, the peace-loving chief did not survive. Approximately 100 of his warriors, plus large numbers of women and children, died that day, after which Custer's men knocked down the tipis and burned the Cheyenne food and supplies. In addition, hundreds of Cheyenne ponies were killed. Custer took a liking to one of the survivors, a beautiful young woman named Monahseetah, daughter of a Cheyenne subchief, and made her his interpreter despite her inability to speak English. A few months later, when Custer returned to his wife at Fort Hayes, Kansas, he left his beautiful Indian maiden behind.[11]

In February 1869, only a few months after the proclamation of the Fort Laramie Treaty, the War Department violated the provision of the agreement that allowed Indians to hunt in the unceded land. It issued a statement declaring that Indians traveling beyond the reservation were subject to military jurisdiction and would be considered hostile. Sitting Bull, of course, was unaware of this directive.[12]

With the Bozeman Trail forts dismantled, Sitting Bull concentrated on the upper Missouri River area.[13] A large number of Sitting Bull's pictographs from this period show his increasing military focus on Euroamericans.[14] Just a few months after the Fort Laramie treaty, Sitting Bull led a raid against Fort Buford in northwest North Dakota, a fort he especially resented. The Hunkpapas killed three soldiers, wounded three others, and captured more than 200 cattle. Sitting Bull followed this action with additional harassing raids against Fort Buford, as well as raids against Forts Rice, Stevenson, and Totten, the latter in the Devil's Lake region of northeast Dakota Territory. Another significant attempt to harm Fort Buford took place in September 1870. With a force of 200 Hunkpapas, Miniconjous, and Cheyennes, Sitting Bull attacked the cattle herd attached to a camp of woodsmen working for Durfee and Peck, the company hired to supply wood to the fort. One of the men, Charles Teck, was driving oxen about 500 yards from the camp and was cut off. Teck made a heroic stand, shooting several of his attackers until he ran out of ammunition. Then he used his rifle as a club but was soon overwhelmed.[15]

After this attack on the woodcutters, Sitting Bull made a strategic decision to adopt a more defensive posture. In Robert Utley's words, he shifted his military policy from being the lance of his people to being their shield.[16] He would fight the Euroamericans but only when they posed an immediate threat to the welfare of the Lakotas.

By this time, the nonreservation Lakota area had shifted westward, pushed by the carving out of reservations toward the east and pulled by the migration of the buffalo to the west. Lakotas now viewed their territory as stretching westward from the Powder River to the Bighorn and north to the Missouri River, then northwest to the Musselshell; however, it was an area not long left to their control.

SITTING BULL MADE SUPREME CHIEF

One of the wisest of the Hunkpapa leaders was Sitting Bull's uncle Four Horns, one of the four tribal chiefs or shirt wearers chosen in 1851. Sitting Bull had been a war chief since 1857 but was not one of these four chiefs. Four Horns recognized that not only had most of the tribal chiefs (Running Antelope, Loud Voiced Hawk, Red Horn, and himself) disappointed their people in various ways,[17] but that resisting the Euroamericans required more unity than the Lakotas had traditionally exercised. A new type of war pitted them against a highly organized enemy, and the Lakotas must adapt, he believed, if they were to survive.

So Four Horns devised a plan to unify all the Sioux still resisting U.S. government expansion under one supreme leader, a plan that actually resulted in demoting himself. That leader was to be Sitting Bull. The war chief was a proven leader, courageous warrior, accomplished hunter, and revered Wichasha Wakan. Widely, although not of course universally, liked, he was the one man, Four Horns believed, who could lead successfully in this new and necessary position.

Although the precise date of Sitting Bull's elevation to supreme leader is uncertain, it likely took place after the Fort Laramie conference, in 1869, on the middle Rosebud Creek in Montana.[18] Present were representatives from the Hunkpapas, Blackfeet, Miniconjous, Sans Arcs, Oglalas, and Cheyennes. Absent were such famed leaders as Red Cloud of the Oglalas and Spotted Tail of the Brulés, both having committed to reservation life. Crazy Horse, the great Oglala war leader, was not only in accord with Sitting Bull but became the Hunkpapa leader's second in command.

The inauguration took place in a specially constructed lodge made from several tipis and open on one side. The four tribal chiefs—Four Horns, Red Horn, Loud Voiced Hawk, and Running Antelope—carried Sitting Bull on a buffalo robe into the council lodge. As at all important events, the ceremonies began with an offering of the sacred pipe to the four corners of the earth and smoking of the pipe by the most prominent individuals present. The pipe, decorated with duck feathers, was then presented to Sitting Bull as a sign of his position. A number of other items were presented to their leader: a bow and 10 arrows, a flintlock gun, a war bonnet with a double tail of eagle feathers that hung to the ground (each feather representing a brave action by the warrior who had supplied it), and a white horse. Astride his new horse, Sitting Bull led a parade of warriors all dressed in their finest clothes, shields uncovered to show their sacred symbolism. As they rode, they chanted songs while circling about the camp. Sitting Bull, the greatest of all the Lakotas, loudly sang a song recalled by those who were present that day and translated into English by Stanley Vestal:

> Ye tribes, behold me.
> The chiefs of old are gone.
> Myself, I shall take courage.[19]

TRADITIONAL ENEMIES

During the end of the 1860s and the early years of the 1870s, Sitting Bull found himself facing both traditional Indian enemies and the advancing Euroamericans. Sitting Bull and his Hunkpapa warriors had one of their most memorable encounters with their traditional Crow adversaries during the winter of 1869–70. Sitting Bull's people were spending the winter along the Missouri River and, to the north of it, Big Dry Creek, in Montana. Two Hunkpapa boys had been out hunting and were returning to camp when a party of Crows discovered them. In a frantic race, the boys tried unsuccessfully to outdistance their pursuers. One was overtaken and killed; the second, although wounded, escaped to tell Sitting Bull of the attack.

The Hunkpapa leader gathered about 100 warriors and set off after the Crows. Assuming that the Hunkpapas would be in pursuit, the Crows took shelter behind a group of rocks on the high ground near Big Dry Creek. Well protected, the Crows fired their guns furiously at the Hunkpapas, who repeatedly charged, fired, mainly using bows and arrows, and withdrew to repeat the charge. As the battle progressed, Sitting Bull reached the rocks and stretched his bow across them, touching three Crows to count coup.

The Crows, 30 in number, finally were killed, but the Hunkpapas suffered heavy casualties in victory. Fourteen Hunkpapas were dead, including the boy returning from hunting and Looks for Him in a Tent, an uncle of Sitting Bull. The Hunkpapa leader, who was fond of his uncle, mourned his death by covering his own face with mud, cutting his hair, and going barefoot in the harsh winter weather.

There was much grieving in the Hunkpapa village over the dead, but the battle nevertheless was celebrated as a major victory, known as the Thirty Crows Killed Battle.[20] Sitting Bull drew a pictograph of his involvement (number 52 shows him wearing a horned hat and counting coup on one of the Crows while the enemy warrior shoots at him), and the event appears in winter counts. A Miniconjou winter count that White Bull assumed responsibility for keeping in 1879 cites the killing of the 30 Crows as the dominant event of 1869.[21]

Another major battle pitted the Hunkpapas of Sitting Bull against the Flatheads in the summer of 1870. The Flatheads lived in western Montana near present-day Flathead Lake. Tribes of the Salishan linguistic group, which included the Flatheads, usually practiced flattening of the head in infancy by strapping babies to hard cradleboards. The flattened back of the head made the top of the head appear rounder than usual. The Flatheads, however, did not practice head deformation, which meant that their heads, being quite normal, actually appeared flat next to other Salishan peoples, who had seemingly rounder heads.[22] The Flatheads also hunted the buffalo and increasingly, from Sitting Bull's point of view, were trespassing on Lakota land, a condition largely forced on them by prospectors who had overrun their traditional hunting grounds.[23]

While camped along the Yellowstone River where it joins the Rosebud, Sitting Bull announced that he was going off by himself to seek a vision. As he was singing, he saw a ball of fire coming toward him. Returning to the camp, he lit his pipe, smoked it, and then announced that he saw in the smoke a battle that would occur in two days and in which enemy Indians as well as some Lakotas would be killed.

Shortly after that, Hunkpapa scouts reported finding a Flathead camp. Sitting Bull took a large force of 400 warriors and set out for it. He decided to use the decoy strategy and sent about 40 men forward to draw the Flatheads out while the main force took up their positions. Before the larger body could prepare for the ambush, however, a Flathead left his camp with some horses. The decoy party immediately charged, capturing horses but allowing the Flathead to rouse his camp.

The Flatheads came out to face the Lakotas and after some fighting, with casualties light on both sides, withdrew to their camp. Most of the attackers also withdrew, but when the Flatheads came out to retrieve their dead, Sitting Bull, his nephew White Bull, his adopted brother Jumping Bull, and a few others attacked. Sitting Bull rode toward one of the Flatheads, who aimed his rifle and shot, wounding him in the left forearm. In another version, the weapon is a bow and arrow, but in either case, Sitting Bull's vision was seen as having come true, with the ball of fire interpreted as the bullet (or arrow). For his wound, Sitting Bull had earned yet another red feather.[24]

NORTHERN PACIFIC RAILROAD

As much as Sitting Bull wanted to be left alone by the Euroamericans, that was not to be. Perhaps the most obtrusive incursion was that of the Northern Pacific Railroad, planned to run directly through Lakota hunting grounds to connect St. Paul, Minnesota, with Seattle, Washington. Trains frightened buffalo, seriously undermining the Lakotas' very survival. U.S. government and military officials knew the provocative nature of the railroad and that the Lakotas surely would resist it. Now that railroad construction was accelerating, in great part because Philadelphia financier Jay Cooke had secured the necessary funding, the government had to find a suitable strategy.[25]

To avoid, or at least postpone, war, Indian Affairs Commissioner Francis A. Walker decided to attempt buying off the tribes that stood in the way of the railroad. The result was the Milk River Agency Initiative, centered at the Milk River Agency in Montana at the Fort Browning trading post north of the Missouri. Large numbers of buffalo in the area proved an effective draw, and the government offered rations in the hope of establishing a more permanent attraction. By the spring of 1871, 6,000 Dakotas from Minnesota and Yanktonais already were encamped at the agency. Lakotas soon arrived, establishing a community of approximately 600 lodges.

Montana Indian Superintendent Jasper A. Viall then sought to entice Sitting Bull into discussions that he hoped might establish peace for the railroad workers. Sitting Bull appears to have been interested in establishing a firmer basis for trading, especially at Fort Peck, which stood at the confluence of the Missouri and Milk Rivers. On September 8, 1871, Sitting Bull arrived at Fort Peck, calling from outside the stockade that he wished to discuss trading. In November, a meeting took place between Andrew J. Simmons, the agent at Milk River Agency, and Lakota representatives who included Black Moon but not Sitting Bull. The discussions proved temporarily effective from the government's perspective, as Sitting Bull spent the 1871–72 winter near Fort Peck.

Hoping that it might be possible to entice Sitting Bull into a permanent relationship, the U.S. Congress appropriated $500,000 in May 1872 for clothing, food, and supplies for the Lakota Sioux who were residing near Fort Peck. With this inducement in hand, Benjamin R. Cowen, Assistant Secretary of the Interior, led a commission to Fort Peck in an attempt to persuade Sitting Bull and other "hostiles" to travel to Washington, D. C., and meet with the President, often referred to by government officials paternalistically as "the Great Father."[26]

Red Cloud had already been in Washington and met with Ulysses S. Grant, who by then had been elected President. On returning to the Plains, Red Cloud sent a message to Sitting Bull urging him to enter into friendship with the U.S. government. After stating his own decision not to engage in any more warfare, he urged, "Make no trouble for our Great Father. His heart is good. Be friends to him and he will provide for you."[27] The admonition, however, carried no weight with Sitting Bull.

By 1872, Sitting Bull's family was growing. His wife, Red Woman, had died in 1871, leaving three children for Sitting Bull to care for, a son by Red Woman and two daughters by the rejected Snow on Her. Although his sister Good Feather helped with the children, Sitting Bull decided that a wife was essential both to help care for his children and because his own status as a leader required the conventional attribute of a wife. Consequently, Sitting Bull successfully offered several horses to Gray Eagle for the right to marry his sister Four Robes.

There also was another sister, Seen by the Nation, a widow with two sons, Little Soldier and Blue Mountain. The latter was a deaf-mute, a condition that did not deter Sitting Bull from also taking Seen by the Nation as a wife to provide for her and her children, another example of Sitting Bull's generosity and compassion. He even gave up his prized war horse, Bloated Jaw, for her. Both women would remain Sitting Bull's wives until his death in 1890. In addition, Sitting Bull's mother, Her Holy Door, had been living with Sitting Bull since her husband's death. Sitting Bull's extensive family responsibilities, however, did not deter him from risking his life to oppose the advancing Euroamericans and their railroad.

In the fall of 1871 when the U.S. cavalry and a party of railroad surveyors appeared along Yellowstone River, what the Lakotas called the Elk River, Sitting Bull paid close attention but did not immediately attack. In the summer of 1872, two additional groups of Northern Pacific engineers returned, accompanied by two sizable military forces: 600 soldiers under Colonel David S. Stanley out of Fort Rice, and 500 soldiers under Major Eugene M. Baker from Fort Ellis near Bozeman, Montana.

In August, warriors from several Lakota tribes had come together at the Powder River in southeastern Montana for a Sun Dance to prepare for a military expedition against their Crow enemies. The large force started moving west to engage the Crows. Then scouts reported soldiers nearby on the north bank of the Yellowstone near the mouth of Arrow Creek. This was Major Baker's troops with 20 railroad workers.

While chiefs discussed whether to continue after Crows or confront the soldiers, a number of young warriors escaped notice of the akicita who were trying to prevent any unsanctioned attacks and made the decision for the chiefs. The soldiers and railroad employees took refuge in a dry riverbank while the Lakotas fired from higher ground and raced "daring lines" past the shooting soldiers.

The encounter, known as the Battle of Arrow Creek, did not prove decisive for either party; and the attackers, faced with the U.S. military's usual superior firepower, withdrew. Yet the railroad employees were so badly shaken by the encounter that they turned northward to the Musselshell River rather than continue down the Yellowstone, returning as quickly as possible to Fort Ellis.[28]

The battle was most memorable for a display of courage by Sitting Bull unlike anything that either Indians or the soldiers had ever seen. It resulted from the need for Sitting Bull to reestablish his authority over the young warriors who were inclined to let their impetuosity overrule their judgment.

According to Sitting Bull's nephew White Bull, a man named Long Holy claimed that he had received the power to protect men from bullets. Long Holy gathered a group of young men around him, including White Bull, who believed his assertion, and explained that to participate in this protection they must follow certain rituals, including use of particular paints and symbols on their faces.

The first serious test of Long Holy's powers came during the battle with Major Baker's troops. Long Holy urged his followers to ride four circles around the soldiers, each circle coming closer to them, and then charge. The stratagem obviously was not working, as the young warriors from the start were suffering wounds. Sitting Bull, recognizing the fallacy of Long Holy's claim and concerned for his nephew and the other warriors, commanded the riders to desist. Long Holy strongly objected, and the two men found themselves in a contest for spiritual and military authority. Finally, the riders obeyed Sitting Bull and withdrew.

At that point Sitting Bull decided to show that the order he gave exhibited no lack of personal bravery on his part. He laid down his weapons and, picking up his pipe and tobacco pouch, strolled into the area between the two warring forces. With bullets kicking up dust around him, he struck fire with his flint and steel, lighted his pipe, and calmly smoked. Then he invited others to join him. White Bull, another Lakota named Gets the Best of Them, and two Cheyennes reluctantly accepted. White Bull recalled the four smoking as fast as they could in order to get out of the open as soon as possible; however, Sitting Bull was in no hurry. After finishing his smoke, he carefully cleaned out his pipe, then returned at a leisurely pace to his amazed fellow Lakotas. The other four raced to safety in such a hurry that Gets the Best of Them forgot his arrows, which White Bull retrieved. It was, according to White Bull, the bravest act ever by Sitting Bull. It certainly reaffirmed Sitting Bull's authority and put Long Holy in his place.[29]

By the summer of 1873, the Northern Pacific Railroad had reached the Missouri River, giving rise to the town of Bismarck, North Dakota. Also that summer, another surveying party set out, moving west from Fort Rice under the protection of soldiers commanded by Colonel Stanley. A large contingent of Hunkpapas and Miniconjous was camped in the party's direct line of movement. Soon, Sitting Bull would encounter Colonel George Custer for the first time.

As the troops and surveyors approached, the Lakotas again attempted the decoy strategy, and it almost succeeded. The decoy party appeared to two companies led by Custer, who followed the Lakotas but pulled up just in time to avoid being wiped out in an ambush. He and his men took refuge in nearby woods and held off their assailants until Stanley appeared.

The Lakotas then withdrew, keeping ahead of the pursuing Custer. When they reached the Yellowstone River, they crossed it in circular bull boats made out of willow frames covered with buffalo hides. Some of the warriors swam their horses across.[30]

Ultimately, the financial panic of 1873 did what Sitting Bull could not accomplish—stop the advance of the Northern Pacific Railroad, although only temporarily. Jay Cooke tried to solicit additional financing by forming a syndicate to sell bonds in exchange for a bonus in stocks, but with the onset of the financial depression in 1873, Cooke was forced to close down his efforts. The failure of Cooke's prestigious Philadelphia banking house triggered a flood of bank and corporation closings. Not until 1879 would the country completely escape from the depression, at which point Frederick Billings, after whom Billings, Montana, was named, assumed the presidency of the railroad, and the Northern Pacific resumed its path westward.[31]

NOTES

1. The Medicine Lodge treaties were signed by members of the Cheyenne, Arapaho, Kiowa, Apache, and Comanche tribes.

2. For Red Cloud and the Fort Laramie Treaty, see Robert W. Larson, "Lakota Chief Red Cloud: Formidable in War and Peace," *Chiefs and Generals: Nine Men Who Shaped the American West*, ed. Richard W. Etulain and Glenda Riley (Golden, CO: Fulcrum Publishing, 2004), 9–10.

3. Much of the following information regarding Father De Smet's peace mission is taken from Stanley Vestal, *Sitting Bull: Champion of the Sioux*, 2nd ed. (1957; Norman: University of Oklahoma Press, 1989), 98–109; Robert Utley, *The Lance and the Shield: The Life and Times of Sitting Bull* (1993; New York: Ballantine Books, 1994), 80–81; and John J. Killoren, *"Come, Blackrobe": De Smet and the Indian Tragedy* (Norman: University of Oklahoma Press, 1994), 318–23.

4. Killoren, 318–19.

5. Killoren, 52.

6. Utley, 255–56; and Jeffrey Ostler, *The Plains Sioux and U.S. Colonialism From Lewis and Clark to Wounded Knee* (New York: Cambridge University Press, 2004), 192–93. For an extended discussion of Sitting Bull and Christianity, see Colin F. Taylor, *Sitting Bull and the White Man's Religion* (Wyk, Germany: Verlag Für Amerikanistik D. Kuegler, 2000).

7. Hiram M. Chittenden and Alfred T. Richardson, eds. *Life, Letters, and Travels of Father Pierre-Jean De Smet, S.J., 1801–1873*, 4 vols. (New York: Francis P. Harper, 1905), 3: 912. For Galpin's journal, see Gilbert J. Garraghan, S.J., "Father De Smet's Sioux Peace Mission of 1868 and the Journal of Charles Galpin," *Mid-America* 13 (1930): 141–63.

8. Vestal, *Sitting Bull*, 108–09.

9. Charles J. Kappler, ed. *Indian Affairs: Laws and Treaties*, 7 vols. (1904–41; Washington, DC: U.S. Government Printing Office, 1975–79), 2: 998–1007.

10. Killoren, 322.

11. Dee Brown, *The American West* (1994; New York: Simon and Schuster, 1995), 106–07.

12. Vestal, *Sitting Bull*, 110.

13. Ostler, 51.

14. Sitting Bull's first pictographic autobiography is known as *The Kimball Pictographic Record* after the physician, Dr. James Kimball, who acquired a copy of the original drawings in 1870. The series is published in *Three Pictographic Autobiographies of Sitting Bull*, edited by M. W. Stirling (Washington, DC: Smithsonian Institution, 1938). See pictographic illustrations 11–12, 14–22, and 25–26.

15. Utley, 90.

16. Utley, 91.

17. Vestal, *Sitting Bull*, 83–85.

18. Utley, 87.

19. Vestal, *Sitting Bull*, 91–95.

20. Vestal, *Sitting Bull*, 113–16; Utley, 97–99.

21. Joseph White Bull, *Lakota Warrior*, trans. and ed. by James H. Howard (1968; Lincoln: University of Nebraska Press, 1996), 21.

22. Bill Yenne, *The Encyclopedia of North American Indian Tribes: A Comprehensive Study of Tribes from the Abitibi to the Zuni* (North Dighton, MA: J. G. Press, 1989), 67. For more detail on the Flatheads, see Harry Holbert Turney-High, *The Flathead Indians of Montana* (Menasha, WI: American Anthropological Association, 1937).

23. Stanley Vestal, *Warpath: The True Story of the Fighting Sioux Told in a Biography of Chief White Bull* (1934; Lincoln: University of Nebraska Press, 1984), 117.

24. Vestal, *Sitting Bull*, 118–24 and *Warpath*, 117–24; Utley, 99–100.

25. Alexander B. Adams, *Sitting Bull: An Epic of the Plains* (New York: G. P. Putnam's Sons, 1973), 213–14.

26. Utley, 93–97.

27. Robert W. Larson, *Red Cloud: Warrior-Statesman of the Lakota Sioux* (Norman: University of Oklahoma Press, 1997), 150.

28. Vestal, *Sitting Bull*, 125–31; Utley, 107–09.

29. For an extensive description of Sitting Bull's performance with the pipe based on White Bull's first-hand account, see Vestal, *Warpath*, 131–44.

30. Utley, 110–12.

31. Adams, 224–25, 241. For a detailed discussion, see M. John Lubetkin, *Jay Cook's Gamble: The Northern Pacific Railroad, the Sioux, and the Panic of 1873* (Norman: University of Oklahoma Press, 2006).

Chapter 5

THE PATH TO LITTLE BIGHORN (1873–1876)

SLOTAS AND FRANK GROUARD

Faced with the prospect of a prolonged and difficult conflict with the U.S. soldiers and others intruding into what he viewed as his lands, Sitting Bull recognized the need for more effective weapons. By 1873, he had begun replacing the old flintlock muskets and rifles that used powder and ball with modern repeating rifles that fired metallic cartridges. Acquiring those weapons, however, was difficult, as most Euroamerican traders refused to trade weapons that might be used against themselves or their own soldiers.

The Slotas, or Métis, of mixed French and Indian descent, lived across the border in Canada.[1] They were experienced traders who transported their goods in heavy two-wheeled wooden carts. Unlike Euroamericans, they had no scruples about trading guns and ammunition to the Lakotas. Although Sitting Bull had no great fondness for Slotas, necessity led him to seek a trading agreement with them.

As a result, the Slotas arrived in the winter of 1872–73 at Sitting Bull's Hunkpapa camp near Dry Fork Creek in central Montana. In addition to weapons and ammunition, the Slotas brought a large supply of whiskey. According to Frank Grouard, who was living in Sitting Bull's camp, the whiskey led to several days of drunkenness on the part of many of the Hunkpapas. Fights broke out, and several Hunkpapas were killed. A faction that opposed Sitting Bull, emboldened by the whiskey, became a serious threat to his life, but Sitting Bull's loyal supporters protected him.

Then, seeing what mischief they had begun, the Slotas left camp in the dark of night.

Grouard, not wanting to be caught up in the hostilities, which could easily have turned against him, rode out of camp and stayed away for three days until things calmed down. As Grouard returned, he could hear the crying of the relatives of those who had been killed.[2]

For several years, Frank Grouard had been a close friend of Sitting Bull's and an adopted family member. The son of a Mormon missionary, Benjamin F. Grouard, and a Polynesian mother, he had been adopted by Addison Pratt, another missionary, and taken to Utah. In 1865, at the age of 15, he ran away to Montana to find a more adventurous life.

Grouard became a mail carrier on the route between Forts Peck and Hall in Montana. The precise date of his capture is given by Vestal as January 2, 1869, although in Grouard's own account he is vague about the specific date.[3] Whatever the precise day, he was riding his route when two Hunkpapa warriors attacked him, knocking him to the ground. Because of the cold weather, Grouard was wearing a heavy buffalo coat with buffalo mitts on his hands and buffalo leggings and moccasins on his legs and feet.

One warrior tried to pull his coat off him while the other attempted to get a clear shot. Then another Indian, clearly a person of authority, rode up and ordered the men to desist. It turned out to be Sitting Bull, who sat down, motioned for the mail carrier to join him, and smoked his pipe for a time. Then Sitting Bull led the captive back to his camp.

Sitting Bull had Grouard sleep in his own tipi while he held a council to decide the prisoner's fate. Most, including Gall and No Neck, wanted to kill him; but Sitting Bull reminded them of his earlier rescue of the young Assiniboine, whom he had adopted as his brother and renamed Jumping Bull, and who by this time was widely respected by the Hunkpapas. Citing this precedent, Sitting Bull declared that the captive would live and be his brother, named Standing Bear.

Grouard notes that for a long time he did not know why Sitting Bull gave him the name Standing Bear, but it proved to be an example of the war chief's sense of humor. Sitting Bull at first mistook Grouard, flailing about in his buffalo coat, for a bear. He soon had another name as well, Grabber, which describes the way a standing bear fights its adversary, by grabbing the opponent within its strong arms.[4]

Grouard became a skilled hunter and marksman while living with the Lakotas. He also learned the country in great detail. Edgar Stewart, who edited Joe DeBarthe's biography of Grouard, wrote that he "probably knew the topography of the Northern Plains better than most men know their own back yard."[5] These skills later would make him one of the West's most famous army scouts. Despite Grouard's later break with Sitting Bull, he retained great respect for the Hunkpapa chief. Years later, he offered the following tribute:

> No man in the Sioux nation was braver in battle than Sitting Bull, and he asked none of his warriors to take any chances that he was not willing at all times to share. I could recall a hundred different instances coming under my own observation to prove Sitting Bull's bravery, and in the first great Sun Dance that I ever witnessed after my capture by the Sioux, I heard Sitting Bull recount his "*coups* in action." They numbered sixty-three, most of them being victories over Indian enemies.[6]

In the spring of 1873, Grouard learned on a trip to Fort Peck of a plan to arrest the Slotas who had sold whiskey to the Hunkpapas. The agent at Fort Peck asked Grouard to help find the Slotas. He decided to do that but had to avoid letting Sitting Bull know what he was planning, so he made up a story about going out to steal horses. Instead, he returned to Fort Peck, led the soldiers to the Slota camp, and identified those responsible for the whiskey sales.

Grouard knew that Sitting Bull would oppose his actions because of the trade agreement with the Slotas and also because he had helped the soldiers. To cover his intention, Grouard asked the troops for some of the Slotas' horses. Returning to the Hunkpapas with three horses, he claimed to have stolen them and gave one each to Sitting Bull, his mother, Her Holy door, and Sitting Bull's sister Good Feather. Unfortunately, two Santees who had been present at the Slota camp arrived and told Sitting Bull what Grouard had done, a revelation that angered Sitting Bull, especially because of his adopted brother's deception. Grouard believed that only the presence of Good Feather and Her Holy Door prevented Sitting Bull from killing him.

His relationship with Sitting Bull continued to be tense, and before long Grouard left the Hunkpapa camp to join Crazy Horse. After approximately two years with Crazy Horse, he decided, in about 1875, to return to his father's people. At that point, in a decision that greatly disappointed and angered Sitting Bull, he started actively working on behalf of the U.S. government.[7]

Sitting Bull would never have aided the soldiers in an engagement with the Slotas, but he was ready to fight his trading partners if they entered Lakota territory without permission. That is precisely what happened in

the late spring of 1873 when a contingent of 200 to 300 Slotas was discovered to have crossed the Yellowstone River. The Hunkpapa attack,
however, did not go well. The Slotas were aware that Sitting Bull was
coming and formed a circle with their wagons. Armed with rifles and a
cannon, they kept their attackers at a distance and then suddenly charged
the Hunkpapas. About eight Hunkpapas died before Sitting Bull led his
men home. One of the dead was Cloud Man, who had been shot from his
horse as he attempted to capture a Slota horse deliberately turned loose
to entice the attackers into the open. Sitting Bull, exhibiting the bravery
and concern for his people that helped make him a popular leader, raced
out to retrieve his fallen warrior.[8]

THE BLACK HILLS

Colonel George Armstrong Custer, his history inextricably bound
to Sitting Bull's through the Battle of Little Bighorn, reappeared in the
Lakotas' lives in the summer of 1874. Rumors of gold in the Black Hills
of the Dakota Territory, an area within the Great Sioux Reservation, had
circulated for some time, and in July, Custer, under the direction of General Philip Sheridan, led an exploratory expedition that included miners and newspaper correspondents. The official reason for the expedition,
perhaps an attempt not to antagonize the Lakotas by threatening their
land granted under the 1868 Fort Laramie Treaty, was that Custer was
merely searching out a good site for a fort that could support the reservation Indians at the Red Cloud and Spotted Tail agencies in northern
Nebraska and also protect the railroad.

Both Custer and the newspapermen wanted something newsworthy,
and the miners were there to find gold, not to fail, although they apparently found little. Private Theodore Ewert was under Custer's command
during the expedition and recorded in his diary that "the earth containing
the precious metal is so scarce that but a very few persons will be the lucky
owners of any." Ewert was correct regarding the miners' discoveries at the
time, but future prospectors did find considerable gold in the Black Hills.
The correspondents, who wanted to please their editors with stories that
would sell papers, sent out glowing reports of the rich deposits just waiting
to be excavated. Custer, always anxious to enhance his fame, proclaimed
"gold among the roots of the grass," and with the economic depression of
1873 still raging, prospectors and mining companies rushed to the area.[9]

The Black Hills were of great importance to the Lakotas. Known as
the Paha Sapa, that is, the Hills that are black, the area also was called a
"Meat Pack" by Sitting Bull because of all the game that lived there. The

Black Hills also offered valleys protected from the wind and a seemingly inexhaustible store of firewood. Lodgepole pine supplied strong, straight poles for tipis. Although Sitting Bull preferred the plains where he could hunt buffalo as his primary home, he valued the Black Hills as a ready supply of food and wood when needed. He also sensed a mystical presence in the hills to which many young Lakota men went for their first vision quest and certainly had no intention of turning them over to the U.S. army or miners.[10]

OTHER CONFLICTS

As miners and settlers rushed into the Black Hills, Sitting Bull was primarily occupied with developments farther west. Sitting Bull's old enemies, the Crows, continued to be an irresistible magnet for hostilities. Sitting Bull's men repeatedly harassed the Crow Agency in southern Montana and stepped up their attacks when the agency, in the summer of 1875, was moved farther away from Fort Ellis, near Bozeman, Montana, to a site about 14 miles south of the Yellowstone near the Stillwater River. Sitting Bull's war parties regularly hit wagon trains hauling supplies for construction of the new agency on the premise that government agents or anyone else assisting the Crows also made themselves enemies of the Lakotas.

Sitting Bull also found himself faced with intrusions into his Montana lands by organized groups determined to make their fortune either by prospecting or trading. In February 1874, a large party of 150 men heavily armed with rifles and two cannons and calling itself the Wagon Road and Prospecting Expedition set out from Bozeman, Montana, down the Yellowstone in search of gold, crossing the iced-over river below the mouth of the Bighorn.

On April 4, Sitting Bull led an attack on the expedition's camp. His force included Makes Room's Miniconjous. Although Sitting Bull led several hundred warriors against the camp, the prospecting expedition, primarily consisting of experienced frontiersmen, was able to repel the attackers. Three times, Sitting Bull attacked but was compelled to retreat.

Many members of the expedition had considerable background in trapping animals and applied some of their trapping tricks to their encounters with the Lakotas. They left pemmican and other food poisoned with strychnine in exposed areas, hoping the Lakotas would eat the deadly food. The intended victims, however, were suspicious and left the food alone.

On another occasion, they prepared a booby trap by digging a false grave containing a howitzer shell rather than a body. They covered the shell with nails and bolts and attached a rope from the primer of the shell to a board marking the grave, hoping that the exploding shell would propel nails and bolts over a wide area, resulting in a large number of casualties. One of the Lakotas pulled the rope and did set off the explosion, but fortunately for the bystanders it did not seriously injure anyone.

The Lakota attacks caused few casualties among the would-be prospectors but took a heavy toll on their livestock. Coupled with bad weather, the fighting led the Yellowstone Wagon Road and Prospecting Expedition to give up and return to Bozeman.[11]

A second Bozeman expedition moved into Lakota land in the summer of 1875 with the intention of building a trading post near the confluence of the Yellowstone and Bighorn Rivers. What made the plan thoroughly unworkable was that the group's leader, Fellows D. Pease, intended to broker a peace between the Lakotas and Crows so that he could trade with both. There was, of course, no chance of bringing the two mortal enemies into a trading pact, but Pease and his party proceeded to build several log huts connected by a protective wall of tall wooden posts.

As Pease constructed his fantasy, the Lakotas and Crows fought a major battle about five miles away. The Crows lost one of their leading chiefs in the encounter, Long Horse, and then headed north, leaving the Lakotas to whittle away at Pease's settlement, gradually killing six members of his party and wounding many more through the winter of 1875–76. Fort Pease, however, remained, a failure in regard to Pease's intent but an annoying presence to Sitting Bull. It would not be completely abandoned until March 1876 when, the original trading plan long since discarded, the site had become a precarious refuge for fewer than 20 wolfers who had to be rescued by a cavalry column out of Fort Ellis.[12]

PEACE WITH THE ASSINIBOINES

Peace between the Lakotas and Crows was unthinkable, but the Assiniboines, or Hohes, were another matter.[13] By 1874, Jumping Bull—also known as Little Assiniboine, Kills Plenty, and Stays Back—had grown into a man of about 30. He also had proven himself a devoted adopted brother to Sitting Bull in the 17 years since Sitting Bull had spared his life.

This successful integration of a Hohe into Sitting Bull's family made the concept of peace with the tribe all the more realistic. So when White Dog, a Hohe chief, visited Sitting Bull in 1874 with the intention of establishing a peaceful relationship between their peoples, Sitting Bull was receptive. The two leaders smoked together and exchanged presents, agreeing to a friendship pact that would last until 1879, when Hohe scouts assisted General Nelson Miles against Sitting Bull.

Shortly after the agreement, however, an incident threatened the new peace. Sitting Bull decided on a raid to steal horses from the Slotas. Reaching them required passing through Hohe territory, which Sitting Bull obviously no longer considered a problem. So Sitting Bull, accompanied by his nephew, One Bull; Iron Claw; and One Bull's wife, White Buffalo Woman, set off on the trip. They crossed the Missouri River near Fort Peck and continued up Little River, passing through Hohe territory and locating a camp that Sitting Bull believed was a group of Slotas.

After praying to Wakantanka for success, Sitting Bull and One Bull, under cover of night, carefully approached the horses tethered at the camp. Iron Claw and White Buffalo Woman remained behind in a stand of timber. One of the Slota horses, the lead mare, had a bell hanging around its neck. Sitting Bull cut the strap holding the bell so that it would not ring when the horses moved and awaken the sleeping Slotas. He then looped a lariat around the mare's nose and mounted on its back.

In the meantime, One Bull had been cutting the hobbles of some of the most desirable of the remaining horses, which, once freed, followed the lead mare. The whole action took only a few minutes. Sitting Bull and One Bull were quickly back at the timber with 10 horses where they reunited with the other two members of their group and set off for home.

Everything seemed to be going perfectly when, the next day, about 20 Hohes attacked. The Lakotas fired back, but they clearly were in a precarious position, badly outnumbered and within Hohe country. Then another party of Hohes arrived, this one led by Chief Red Stone. Red Stone knew well who Sitting Bull was and assured him that the Hohes would cause no further trouble. To make sure, Red Stone accompanied Sitting Bull and his group part of the way home.

In an ironic twist to this incident, Big Darkness, a Hohe who remembered the event, later told Stanley Vestal that Sitting Bull had mistakenly raided a Cree camp, mistaking the Crees for Slotas.[14]

THE GREAT SUN DANCE OF 1875

Continuing to face traditional Indian enemies as well as a variety of newer adversaries, including soldiers, miners, and settlers, Sitting Bull tried again to create a more unified force in the summer of 1875. The agent of unification was an especially large Sun Dance that, Sitting Bull hoped, would more closely bind together his Hunkpapas, Spotted Eagle's Sans Arcs, Oglalas led by Crazy Horse and Black Twin, the Miniconjous of Makes Room and White Bull, and the Northern Cheyenes led by Little Wolf and a revered holy man named Ice.

Sitting Bull was both the primary force behind this remarkable Sun Dance and the principal performer at it. Ice had given him a black war horse, and Sitting Bull rode this mighty horse to the Sun Dance lodge. Streaks of white adorned the horse, and Sitting Bull, wearing only a breechcloth, moccasins, and war bonnet, had painted his own body with yellow clay. Strips of black paint covered his forehead and portions of his face, including his chin. His wrists and ankles were circled by black bands, and a black disk on his chest and a black crescent on his right shoulder representing the sun and moon indicated that he had received visions and been in communication with the gods. All of this created an extraordinarily dramatic spectacle, with the black on Sitting Bull's face symbolizing his past success in battle and the yellow covering his body representing destruction and violence. Those watching knew full well that war was not far away.[15]

Sitting Bull danced into the lodge, leading the black horse. He then ordered two pipes filled, one representing Lakotas, the other Cheyennes. Sitting Bull took both pipes and lifted them toward the sacred Sun Dance pole. Then, while those in attendance sang, he danced toward the pole and away from it several times, representing attacks on an enemy. All the while, he continued leading his horse and holding the pipes. Finally, he opened his arms wide and closed them against his chest, encircling his enemies. He then elevated the two pipes, offering them to Wakantanka. Once again, as during his pipe-smoking exhibition of personal bravery in front of enemy troops three years earlier, Sitting Bull knew precisely the combination of spectacle, bravado, and courage that would inspire his people and strengthen his leadership position for the difficult times ahead.

BARGAINING FOR THE BLACK HILLS

By 1875, prospectors seeking their fortune had overrun much of the southern portion of the Black Hills. Although the military had made a half-hearted effort to keep people out, largely to avoid stretching their forces too thin by having to protect them, their efforts had limited success.[16] U.S. public opinion strongly favored opening up the area, and the government sought ways to do that with minimal Indian opposition. The treaties of 1868 unmistakably prevented such incursions on land granted to the tribes as part of the Sioux Reservation, so to government officials, a legal answer, if not required, was at least desirable.

Even the reservation Lakotas, including Red Cloud, opposed turning over the Black Hills, but the primary obstacle, government officials realized, consisted of the so-called hunting bands, the groups, including Sitting Bull's Hunkpapas, who had not agreed to accept reservation life. And by this time, one leader stood out among all the Plains Indians—Sitting Bull.

Consequently, the U.S. government established a commission led by Senator William Boyd Allison of Iowa to negotiate with the tribes for the Black Hills. The government ideal was to purchase the region or, failing that, to lease the hills in a long-term arrangement. A contingent of about 100 agency Indians accompanied by Frank Grouard arrived at Sitting Bull's camp in August 1875 to invite him and others resisting accommodation with the government to attend a council at Red Cloud Agency in northwestern Nebraska to be held in September. After the Sun Dance, the large village had moved to the Tongue River, likely near the state border in southeastern Montana northwest of present-day Sheridan, Wyoming.

Sitting Bull was shocked and angered to learn that Grouard, the Grabber, who in his opinion had betrayed his friendship, was among the peace delegates. According to Grouard, Sitting Bull sent for him, but Grouard, fearing for his life, took Crazy Horse, with whom he still had a good relationship, with him to Sitting Bull's lodge. Grouard urged Sitting Bull to attend the meeting at Red Cloud Agency.

At a council meeting the next morning, a series of speakers opposed going in to the agency. Crazy Horse refused even to talk about the invitation, leaving Little Hawk to speak on his behalf. Sitting Bull, according to Grouard, gave a long speech in which he declared that he was no agency Indian, would never sell the Black Hills, and was prepared for war: "He told me to go out and tell the white men at Red Cloud that he declared open war and would fight them wherever he met them from that time on. His entire harangue was an open declaration of war." [17]

That night, again according to Grouard, a large group of Lakotas decided to kill the delegates, including Grouard. Learning of the plot, Crazy Horse summoned the plotters and warned them not to harm any of the visitors because they were obliged to safeguard anyone invited into the camp as a guest. He then made the consequences of proceeding clear, promising, "'My friends, whoever attempts to murder these people will have to fight me, too.'" Grouard and the rest of his party, however, prudently left camp as soon as possible. For his efforts, Grouard received $500, the first money he had earned since being captured by the Lakotas, money he later said he used partly to buy white man's clothing to replace the Indian clothing he was still wearing. [18]

About 400 Indians did travel to Red Cloud Agency for the council with the Allison Commission, although, among the reservation Indians, they formed only a tiny percentage of those present. Missing, of course, were precisely the leaders Senator Allison and his group most wanted and needed to see.

During the proceedings, Little Big Man, an Oglala, led what Robert Utley referred to as a "mock charge" toward the commissioners, firing rifles and frightening both Indians and government officials alike.[19] At least some of those present thought that it might be the real thing. According to both General George Crook and Lieutenant John Bourke, a large contingent of nonagency Indians led by Little Big Man was ready to wipe out the commissioners but was turned aside by some decisive action that prevented what might have been a massacre. Crook praised the Brulé chief Spotted Tail for stopping the confrontation, whereas Bourke gave the credit to two army officers named Egan and Crawford who formed their men into a line with carbines at the ready to protect the commissioners.[20]

No violence occurred at the Red Cloud Agency council, but no agreements were formed either. Disappointed commissioners returned to Washington and urged Congress to ascertain a fair price for the Black Hills and announce the purchase as an accomplished fact. That, of course, could not be accomplished without major fighting.

THE ULTIMATUM

After the failure of the Allison Commission to secure an agreement to buy or lease the Black Hills, President Ulysses Grant met on November 3 with a number of prominent government officials, including Secretary of the Interior Zachariah Chandler, Commissioner of Indian Affairs Edward P. Smith, Secretary of War William W. Belknap, and Generals Philip Sheridan and George Crook. Grant came to two major decisions. He would retain the prohibition on miners moving into the Black Hills but not enforce the edict. Second, he authorized forcing the hunting bands to yield the unceded land (a clear violation of the 1868 treaty) and settle on the reservation. Implicit within these decisions was the transfer of responsibility for the hostile bands from Indian Affairs to the military, a position that Commanding General of the U.S. Army William Tecumseh Sherman and General Sheridan had been urging.

Grant, either at the same November 3 meeting or later, ordered or at least approved giving the tribes a deadline to enter the reservation, after which they would be considered hostile and be subject to military force to compel their acquiescence. The date chosen was January 31, 1876. On December 6, Commissioner Smith directed the Sioux agents to send runners out to inform the various villages of this directive.

Much political planning went into placing the responsibility for military action on the Indian bands that supposedly were refusing to comply with an official governmental order. Contributing to this perception of Indian responsibility was a report by Erwin Curtis Watkins, one of the Indian inspectors charged with routine investigations of Indian agents' financial and administrative practices. Watkins, who had served with Sheridan and Crook in the Civil War and was a political associate of Chandler, may either have written or merely signed the report. It helped give political cover to the military plan that his friends and the President of the United States wanted to carry out by describing supposed depredations by the Lakotas and urging a military campaign during the winter against them.[21]

The time frame given the tribes was completely unrealistic. The messengers were sent out during a particularly harsh winter, so obeying the order, even if the tribes had wished to do so, would have been physically impossible. The message reached some bands at least as late as December 22; some villages, in fact, were never informed.

To comply would have meant a forced march over hundreds of miles through blizzards and deep snow with women, children, and hungry, weakened horses. Stanley Vestal quotes Sitting Bull's nephew White Bull as sarcastically noting, "'Maybe, if we had had automobiles, we could have made it.'"[22] In addition, even if Sitting Bull and the other Lakotas had reached the agencies, they would have found little or no food there, as famine caused in part by failure to secure the necessary beef herds had hit most agencies by the middle of the winter.

Before the January 31 deadline, General Sheridan had issued orders to prepare for war, no doubt hoping to catch his prey in their camps, where they would have to protect their women and children while trying to fight the attacking army. Sheridan apparently expected a reasonably easy victory. Nature and Sitting Bull, however, would prove far more difficult to defeat than the general anticipated.

NOTES

1. For additional information on the Métis, see Gerhard J. Ens, *Homeland to Hinterland: The Changing Worlds of the Red River Métis in the Nineteenth Century* (Toronto: University of Toronto Press, 1996).

2. Joe DeBarthe, *Life and Adventures of Frank Grouard*, ed. Edgar I. Stewart (Norman: University of Oklahoma Press, 1958), 48–49.

3. Stanley Vestal, *Sitting Bull: Champion of the Sioux*, 2nd ed. (1957; Norman: University of Oklahoma Press, 1989), 111; DeBarthe, 30.

4. DeBarthe, 30–41.

5. DeBarthe, xvi.

6. DeBarthe, 48.

7. DeBarthe, 49–52.

8. Robert M. Utley, *The Lance and the Shield: The Life and Times of Sitting Bull* (1993; New York: Ballantine Books, 1994), 103–04.

9. *Private Theodore Ewert's Diary of the Black Hills Expedition of 1874*, ed. John M. Carroll (Piscataway, NJ: Consultant Resources Incorporated, 1976), 57–58. For accounts of the expedition, see Vestal, 132–33; Utley, 115–16; Charles M. Robinson III, *The Plains Wars 1757–1900* (Osceola, WI: Osprey Publishing, 2003), 58; Jeffrey Ostler, *The Plains Sioux and U.S. Colonialism from Lewis and Clark to Wounded Knee* (New York: Cambridge University Press, 2004), 59–61; Donald Dean Jackson, *Custer's Gold: The United States Cavalry Expedition of 1874* (1966; Lincoln: University of Nebraska Press, 1972); and Ernest Grafe and Paul Horsted, *Exploring with Custer: The 1874 Black Hills Expedition*, 3rd ed. (Custer, SD: Golden Valley Press, 2005).

10. Utley, 115; and Linea Sundstrom, "The Sacred Black Hills: An Ethnohistorical Review," *Great Plains Quarterly* 17 [Summer/Fall] (1997), 185–212.

11. Utley, 118–19.

12. Utley, 119–20, 128.

13. For a firsthand, nineteenth-century account of the Assiniboines (Hohes), see Edwin Thompson Denig, *The Assiniboine*, ed. J.N.B. Hewitt (Regina: Canadian Plains Research Center, 2000).

14. This account of the peace agreement and Sitting Bull's raid is based on Vestal, 134–37.

15. See Utley, 122–13, for details of the Sun Dance; and James R. Walker, *Lakota Belief and Ritual*, ed. Raymond J. DeMallie and Elaine A. Jahner (1980; Lincoln: University of Nebraska Press, 1991), 274–80, for the symbolism.

16. Ostler, 59.

17. DeBarthe, 85–86.

18. DeBarthe, 86.

19. Utley, 126.

20. George Crook, *General George Crook: His Autobiography*, ed. Martin F. Schmitt (Norman: University of Oklahoma Press, 1946), 189–90; John G. Bourke, *On the Border with Crook* (New York: Charles Scribner's Sons, 1891), 243.

21. John S. Gray, *Centennial Campaign: The Sioux War of 1876* (Ft. Collins, CO: The Old Army Press, 1976), 23–31; Utley, 127; and Vestal, 138–39.

22. Vestal, 139.

Sitting Bull, wearing his Strong Heart Society headdress and holding the shield given him by his father, is wounded in the foot while killing a Crow chief in 1856. The image of a sitting buffalo is Sitting Bull's signature in this early pictograph, from one of his pictographic autobiographies. Smithsonian Miscellaneous Collections, vol. 97, no. 5.

Lieutenant Colonel George Armstrong Custer poses for a formal portrait shortly before his death in 1876. Denver Public Library, Western History Collection, Creator D. F. Barry, B-59.

While leading his people back into Canada in 1879, Sitting Bull kills a Crow scout who had advanced far ahead of General Miles. By the time of this pictograph, which appeared in one of his autobiographies, Sitting Bull has learned to sign his name in English. Smithsonian Miscellaneous Collections, vol. 97, no. 5.

In 1882, Sitting Bull's nephew, One Bull, posed for this studio portrait holding a war club. Denver Public Library, Western History Collection, Creator Bailey, Dix & Mead, X-31837.

Sitting Bull, shown here in a photograph taken around 1883, is surrounded clockwise by his mother, Her Holy Door; a sister, Good Feather; a daughter, Walks Looking; and another daughter, Many Horses, who holds her son, Tom Fly. State Historical Society of North Dakota A-2952.

Sitting Bull poses in the mid-1880s for a portrait holding a peace pipe and wearing a crucifix probably given him by Father De Smet. Denver Public Library, Western History Collection, Creator D. F. Barry, B-77.

This picture of Sitting Bull's camp at Standing Rock Agency in the mid-1880s shows horses grazing and hides drying on racks. Denver Public Library, Western History Collection, Creator D. F. Barry, B-773.

"Foes in '76, Friends in '85": In this 1885 publicity photo, Buffalo Bill Cody seemingly points out something in the distance to Sitting Bull. Denver Public Library, Western History Collection, Creator W. Notman, NS-196.

Sitting Bull, left of the monument, and James McLaughlin in top hat and tails to its right participate in a dedication ceremony at Standing Rock Reservation in 1886. Denver Public Library, Western History Collection, Creator D. F. Barry, B-342.

Sitting Bull's wives, Seen by the Nation and Four Robes, and two daughters stand outside Sitting Bull's cabin on Standing Rock Reservation in the late 1880s. Denver Public Library, Western History Collection, Creator D. F. Barry, B-792.

Annie Oakley, "Little Sure Shot," became a close friend of Sitting Bull during their time together with Buffalo Bill's Wild West Show. Here she appears in an 1890s publicity shot. Denver Public Library, Western History Collection, Creator Elliott & Fry, Z-330.

In an undated photograph, Red Tomahawk, credited with killing Sitting Bull, poses at the left next to another reservation policeman, Eagle Man, who was also involved in the attempt to arrest Sitting Bull in 1890. Denver Public Library, Western History Collection, Creator D. F. Barry, B-836.

In a photograph dating from the 1920s, markers show where U.S. soldiers died, and a large stone monument sits atop the hill where Custer and his men made their "last stand" at the Battle of Little Bighorn. Denver Public Library, Western History Collection, Creator F. J. Angier, X-31577.

Chapter 6

THE BATTLE OF LITTLE BIGHORN (1876)

THE CENTENNIAL YEAR

The year 1876 marked the one-hundredth anniversary of the United States, the country having recently survived a wrenching civil war and become, supposedly, once again "one nation indivisible."[1] Pride and optimism abounded among much of the population, and the nation prepared to throw a magnificent party to celebrate its great achievements during its first century of existence. The Centennial International Exhibition, funded by Philadelphia (the city that had witnessed the birth of the nation), the state of Pennsylvania, and the United States Congress, opened on May 10.

President Ulysses S. Grant summarized those areas of national achievement in his speech at the opening of the Centennial Exhibition in Philadelphia's Fairmount Park:

> One hundred years ago our country was new and but partially settled. Our necessities have compelled us to chiefly expend our means and time in felling forests, subduing prairies, building dwellings, factories, ships, docks, warehouses, roads, canals, machinery. Most of our schools, churches, libraries, and asylums have been established within a hundred years. Burdened by these great primal works of necessity, which could not be delayed, we yet have done what this Exhibition will show in the direction of rivaling older and more advanced nations in law, medicine, and theology; in science, literature, philosophy,

and the fine arts. Whilst proud of what we have done, we regret that we have not done more.[2]

Grant did not mention that residing in those subdued prairies were a variety of Indian peoples, among them Sitting Bull's Hunkpapas, and, in fact, that quite a lot of them were still not subdued. And while Grant correctly noted a wide range of areas in which the young country had expressed its ideas, ingenuity, and artistry, only a few of the areas were actually on exhibit for the world to see. Theology, philosophy, and literature, for example, largely gave way to the power of technology.

Some ten million visitors (out of a national population of about fifty million) marveled at the nation's wonders, and since this was an international event, befitting the growing importance of the United States within the family of nations, it also featured exhibits from abroad. Those exhibits included European paintings and sculptures of nudes that shocked the American moral sense and precipitated many a sermon railing against the immorality of the Exhibition gallery.

The most awe-inspiring object at the Centennial was the mammoth Corliss engine that with the turning of two levers (one by President Grant, the other by special guest Dom Pedro, Emperor of Brazil) set into motion thirteen acres of machinery within the Machinery Hall. Less noticed was a small apparatus invented by Alexander Graham Bell that would transform communications forever. An early Remington typewriter (the Remington Typographic Machine) also was on display. Nonmechanical displays featured such products as Hires Root Beer and Heinz Ketchup.[3]

As President Grant presided at the opening of the six-month run of this encomium on American greatness, military forces were in the field preparing to complete the subduing of the plains to which the president had alluded. By the time that Grant closed the Exhibition on November 10, declaring the festivities ended, and the great Corliss engine ground to a halt, he had to feel much less optimistic. Mired in scandals that had besmirched his presidency, he also saw Reconstruction in the South (a process of democratization that Grant strongly supported) grinding to a halt, placing the region under the rule of white supremacists and their Jim Crow laws.[4] In addition, Grant had seen his beloved military suffer, in the Battle at the Little Bighorn, the worst defeat in its history.

WINTER PLANS

January 31, 1876, the deadline for hostile Indian bands to report to government agencies, passed with Sitting Bull still cherishing his freedom.

The Lakotas apparently failed to recognize how seriously the United States government took the deadline, although, as noted in the previous chapter, the harsh winter weather would have precluded their reaching the agencies even if they had tried. General Philip Sheridan, however, had the deadline very much in mind and was planning to march quickly against the tribes once it passed.

General Sheridan, who from his headquarters in Chicago commanded the Military Division of the Missouri, which included all of the plains, wired General Crook and General Alfred Terry on February 8 that the War Department had ordered military action against hostile Indians. Sheridan envisioned a multi-pronged action. Crook would move from Fort Fetterman in Wyoming against Crazy Horse, who was believed to be in the vicinity of the headwaters of the Bighorn, Powder, Rosebud, and Tongue Rivers in northcentral Wyoming. Terry's forces would converge from the east and west, one column under Colonel John Gibbon moving eastward from Fort Ellis in Montana, a second column under Lieutenant Colonel George Armstrong Custer departing Fort Abraham Lincoln in northern Dakota Territory and moving toward the west.

These three forces would encircle the recalcitrant Lakotas and Cheyennes and crush them. From the perspective of the army, that meant finally defeating Sitting Bull and Crazy Horse, the two chiefs best known to the military and to the general American public. In fact, a number of other important leaders were allied with them, but the military was correct in identifying Sitting Bull and Crazy Horse as the two greatest war leaders of the northern Plains tribes.

The planned winter campaign, however, quickly turned at best into a spring campaign, removing the real advantage that Sheridan saw in attacking the tribes during their winter encampment. The bitter winter weather that would have precluded compliance with the January 31 directive also prevented Terry from moving forward. His troops were inadequately provisioned for the lengthy march that would be required to reach Sitting Bull and would have to await a spring thaw to permit more supplies to arrive by train on the Northern Pacific Railroad or by steamship.[5]

POWDER RIVER BATTLE

As General Terry awaited spring, General Crook prepared to move against Crazy Horse, or so he thought. With snow blanketing the land and blizzards bringing more, Crook finalized his plans. Colonel Joseph J. Reynolds (formerly a major general in the volunteer army during the Civil War) would command the expedition, with Crook accompanying him as an observer. Crook's force included six battalions, each including two companies and its own pack train of 50 mules and 62 civilian packers. The total military contingent numbered 662 enlisted men and 30 officers. Also in the party was a supply train of 80 wagons handled by 84 teamsters and five ambulances, each with a driver. Finally, 31 guides and scouts included Frank Grouard. This substantial force departed Fort Fetterman in western Wyoming at the end of February.

Two days out, they lost their beef herd to Indians. With Crook quickly reassuming operational direction of the troops, the force continued trying to locate Crazy Horse. By March 15, scouts thought that they had found the direction in which Crazy Horse was moving. Grouard was convinced that they would find Lakotas on Powder River, about forty miles from Crook's present location.

Crook named Reynolds to head the strike force, which would consist of six companies totaling approximately 370 men. Grouard led the way, at times dropping to his knees to find evidence of the Lakotas' movement. By about six A.M. on March 17, Grouard had found a village on Powder River in southeastern Montana just a few miles above the Wyoming border. One battalion under Captain Henry Noyes would attack. Captain Alexander Moore was in charge of a support battalion, and Captain Anson Mills led a battalion that would be held in reserve. Nothing, however, went right under Reynolds' direction. The rugged terrain slowed down Noyes, who did not reach his attack position until nine o'clock. Moore failed completely to position his battalion on the assigned bluff overlooking the village, and Reynolds was slow in ordering Mills to enter the battle.

The villagers, numbering about 735 people, including approximately 200 warriors, quickly fled with few casualties. A large number of Lakota warriors scaled nearby bluffs and assumed positions that could have proved disastrous for one of Noyes' companies had not Mills' reserves finally arrived to save them.

Although Reynolds had captured the village, it turned out not to be Crazy Horse's. The soldiers suffered four dead and six wounded, with one Lakota and one Cheyenne killed. Much destruction was done to the village, and some seven hundred horses were captured, about one-half of the villagers' herd. The attack, from the military's standpoint, however, was disappointing and would quickly prove even more so. Warriors from the village pursued the troops and that night reclaimed about 550 of the horses.[6]

A disgusted General Crook preferred court-martials against Reynolds, Moore, and Noyes "for misbehavior before the enemy." All three were later convicted, with Reynolds suspended from rank and command for one year, Moore suspended from command for six months, and Noyes formally reprimanded.[7]

SITTING BULL AND THE GATHERING OF THE BANDS

The Powder River villagers, having lost their tipis, robes, and personal possessions, would have faced a disastrous winter were it not for the generosity of Crazy Horse and Sitting Bull. Crazy Horse provided what assistance he could, but his small village was not able to accommodate the large number of refugees left homeless by Crook's attack. They continued farther up the Powder River and about fifty miles east of it reached Sitting Bull's village near Chalk Butte, where they were accorded shelter, food, clothing, and horses. Wooden Leg, a Cheyenne, later recalled that Sitting Bull's Hunkpapas "flooded us with gifts of everything needful. Crowds of their men and women were going among us to find out and to supply our wants." Wooden leg added, "Oh, what good hearts they had! I never can forget the generosity of Sitting Bull's Uncpapa [sic] Sioux on that day."[8]

As spring arrived, increasing numbers of hunting bands migrated to Sitting Bull. The attack at Powder River demonstrated that the United States military was serious about waging war on those who had not joined the reservations, and the Lakotas and their allies knew that they would have to meet the danger with great force. By June 7, according to statistics compiled by John S. Gray and published in his *Centennial Campaign: The Sioux War of 1876*, the village had grown to 461 tipis, often referred to as lodges. Sitting Bull's Hunkpapas were the most numerous group, with 154 lodges. The Cheyennes numbered 100 lodges, with 70 lodges of Crazy Horse's Oglalas and 55 each of Miniconjous and Sans Arcs. Also residing in Sitting Bull's village were small numbers of Blackfeet, Brulés, Yanktonais, and Inkpaduta's Dakotas.[9] This gravitation to Sitting Bull is explained clearly by Wooden Leg's assessment of the great war chief:

> Sitting Bull had come into notice as the most consistent advocate of the idea of living out of all touch with white people. He would not go to the reservation nor would he accept any rations or other gifts coming from the white man government. He rarely went to the trading posts. Himself and his followers were wealthy in food and clothing and lodges, in everything needful to an Indian. They did not lose any horses nor other property in warfare, because they had not any warfare. He had come now into admiration by all Indians as a man whose medi-

cine was good—that is, as a man having a kind heart and good judgment as to the best course of conduct. He was considered as being altogether brave, but peaceable. He was strong in religion—the Indian religion. He made medicine many times. He prayed and fasted and whipped his flesh into submission to the will of the Great Medicine. So, in attaching ourselves to the Uncpapas we other tribes were not moved by a desire to fight. They had not invited us. They simply welcomed us. We supposed that the combined camps would frighten off the soldiers. We hoped thus to be freed from their annoyance. Then we could separate again into the tribal bands and resume our quiet wandering and hunting.[10]

This long analysis by a member of another tribe surely is one of the most remarkable encomiums on an individual ever uttered. It shows the wide range of positive attributes that Sitting Bull possessed and the deep respect that his own Hunkpapas and other tribes had for him. He was seen as a holy man as well as a leader who provided for his own people, caring for both their spiritual and material needs. He was brave yet peaceful. He did not seek war but rather to be left alone to live as his ancestors had lived. In Sitting Bull, Wooden Leg saw no hotheaded chief yearning after combat but a wise and generous leader who would do whatever he judged to be in the best interest of his people.

So as the United States military prepared for what it hoped would be the final victory over Sitting Bull and the Plains Indians, the hunting bands gathered around their greatest leader. Such a large village had to move regularly to find new grazing for the horses and new supplies of game for the villagers. Every few days, this growing contingent of Plains Indians moved toward a new camping ground. The Cheyennes moved at the head and the Hunkpapas at the end, the two largest tribes occupying the two most dangerous, and therefore most honored, positions. Two Moon, selected by his Cheyennes to lead them in war, led his tribe.[11] When the various groups reached the next campsite, they formed six large circles, each opening toward the east, as did each individual tipi. In addition to the rising sun lighting the interior of the tipi, the Spirit of the East, which, they believed, arrives with the sun and presides over the day, would touch the tipi's inhabitants.[12]

During these movements, soldiers were sighted twice. Scouts discovered soldiers north of the Yellowstone River in early May. The force was Colonel Gibbon's out of Fort Ellis. Accompanying Gibbon were twenty-five Crow scouts. Sitting Bull had no desire to attack Gibbon, but many of his young warriors looked fondly on the Crows' thirty-three ponies. During the night, fifty warriors crossed the water to the island in the Yellowstone on which the ponies were grazing and made off with all of them.[13]

A few weeks later, in early June, about a dozen Cheyenne scouts under Little Hawk discovered the camp of General Crook, who had continued northward. They considered stampeding the soldiers' horses in an effort to steal them but concluded, according to Wooden Leg, who was in the party, that the effort would be too dangerous. Several soldiers spotted the Cheyenne scouts and initially believed themselves to be under attack by a large number of Crazy Horse's men.[14]

SOLDIERS FALLING UPSIDE DOWN

Somewhere between May 21 and 24 while camped on the Rosebud, Sitting Bull felt an unseen force pulling him to a nearby butte.[15] When he reached the top, he prepared through prayer and meditation to receive a message from Wakantanka. Then he fell asleep and dreamed of a dust storm rushing toward a white cloud. The cloud he recognized as a Lakota village near a snow-covered mountain, and behind the storm he saw soldiers. As the storm hit the cloud, lightning streaked through the sky and rain poured down. Yet after the storm had vanished, the cloud remained unscathed and drifted off beyond his sight.

Returning to his village, Sitting Bull recalled the dream for the other chiefs and interpreted it according to the wisdom he had received from Wakantanka. The cloud represented his village, which soldiers would attack. But the soldiers would be defeated. Accordingly, directions were given to the scouts, also known as wolves, to watch carefully for the soldiers that Sitting Bull was certain would soon come.

Perhaps a week later, near the end of May, Sitting Bull asked his nephew White Bull, his adopted brother Jumping Bull, and a son of his friend Chief Black Moon to accompany him to the top of a hill. There Sitting Bull, having prepared by loosening the braids of his hair, removing his feathers, and washing off the red paint he often wore on his face, prayed. He asked that Wakantanka provide sufficient food for his people during the coming winter and inspire the Lakota bands to get along well together. In return, Sitting Bull would offer a whole buffalo and dance the Sun Dance. Sitting Bull and his three companions then performed a pipe-smoking ceremony.

Sitting Bull immediately set about fulfilling his promises. In addition to shooting three buffalo and offering the fattest one to Wakantanka, Sitting Bull began organizing a Sun Dance with Black Moon presiding and Sitting

Bull himself as the chief dancer. Only Hunkpapas would participate in this dance, but members of the other bands were permitted to observe.

The usual preparatory ceremonies began about June 4. Once they were completed, Sitting Bull was ready to make a special offering of one hundred pieces of his flesh. He sat with his back against the sacred Sun Dance pole while Jumping Bear knelt beside him. Starting near one of Sitting Bull's wrists and working his way up to near the shoulder, Jumping Bull fifty times inserted a small awl under the skin, lifted the skin flap, and cut off a piece of flesh with his knife. Then Jumping Bull repeated the process fifty times on Sitting Bull's other arm. The pain must have been excruciating for Sitting Bull, and his arms, covered in blood, began to swell badly.

Despite the condition of his arms, Sitting Bull began to dance. This time he chose not to suspend himself from the pole, but onlookers could readily see the scars on his chest and back from at least one earlier dance when he had been suspended.

For the rest of the day and that night, and into the next day, Sitting Bull danced, staring into the sun during daylight hours. Finally, he stopped, appearing to have passed out on his feet. Hunkpapas gently lowered him to the ground and brought him water.

When Sitting Bull revived, he told Black Moon of the vision he had received, and Black Moon shared it with the rest of the assembly. Sitting Bull had seen large numbers of soldiers, as thick as grasshoppers, descending from the sky into his camp, but they and their horses were falling upside down. The voice that Sitting Bull heard in his vision announced that the soldiers had no ears, meaning that they failed to hear what Sitting Bull had been saying about leaving his people alone. The upside-down image meant that the soldiers would be killed, but the victors were cautioned in the vision not to take any plunder. Some Indians also appeared upside down, indicating that Sitting Bull and his people would also suffer fatalities. However, the battle would be a great victory for Sitting Bull and his warriors.

The vision would soon prove prophetic, but it also helped pave the way for victory. Sitting Bull's vision increased the Indians' confidence regarding the impending battle and, coupled with his remarkable demonstration of self-sacrifice during the Sun Dance, must have erased any doubts about Sitting Bull's leadership.

BATTLE OF THE ROSEBUD

As Sitting Bull was inspiring his followers with his historic vision, General George Crook was preparing to move north from the Sheridan,

Wyoming, area in search of hostiles. By June 15, reports had come to Crook that a large village was within about forty-five miles of his present location. Believing that the expedition would be short, Crook decided to take only four days' worth of rations and leave his pack train behind.[16]

Crook departed early in the morning of June 16 with 100 soldiers, 85 volunteers in support roles, and 262 Indian allies consisting of Shoshones, Crows, and Arikaras (also known as Rees). Wanting to move rapidly, he mounted his 175 infantrymen on 175 wagon mules, which the infantry-men had first attempted to ride only the day before. Crook's troops fol-lowed Goose Creek to Tongue River, crossed it, and proceeded the few additional miles to Montana. They then moved northwest toward the Rosebud River, believing that the main enemy camp was nearby. It was not, for Sitting Bull was already moving for the fourth time since the Sun Dance, heading gradually toward the Little Bighorn in pursuit of buffalo. By the evening of June 16, he had camped at Reno Creek between the Rosebud and Little Bighorn.

Crook's movements had not gone unnoticed. Little Hawk and his scouts had observed soldiers advancing toward the Rosebud. While Crook slept on the south fork of the Rosebud, a Sioux and Cheyenne force moved toward him. The intent was to prevent the soldiers from reaching the vil-lage and endangering everyone there.

Reveille brought the soldiers to order at 3:00 in the morning of June 17. By 6:00, the column was moving, preceded by Crow scouts. Crook soon reached the main branch of the Rosebud. By 8:00, Crook had ordered his men to stop. The men unsaddled their mounts, and Crook and some of his officers played whist while his men drank coffee.

Crook, a veteran Indian fighter who had enjoyed considerable success against the Apaches in the Southwest, was proud of his reputation for never having lost a battle. Known as "Three Stars" by the Indians, he was also very conscious of his image, wearing a canvas suit and cork helmet rather than the traditional uniform, and sporting a forked beard braided with the two ends tied behind his neck.

Suddenly, shooting could be heard beyond bluffs to the north. Some 750 warriors led by Sitting Bull and Crazy Horse had encountered a party of Crook's scouts. The remaining scouts rushed to engage the attackers. The soldiers quickly organized themselves and also entered the battle.

The fighting raged furiously, first between the two sets of Indians, then between Sitting Bull's warriors and Crook's entire force. The Sioux and Cheyennes attacked, withdrew, and then counterattacked when the enemy spread apart in pursuit.

Then Crook, mistakenly believing that the enemy camp was nearby on the Rosebud, ordered two battalions, Captain Mills' Third Cavalry and Captain Noyes' Second Cavalry, to withdraw from the fighting and proceed to the village. Frank Grouard argued against the maneuver because it would take the cavalry down a canyon whose walls were covered with vegetation that could conceal an ambush. Nonetheless, before noon, Mills was following Crook's orders and moving through the canyon when Adjutant A. H. Nickerson caught up to him with new orders. The ferocity of the main battle required Mills to bring his men back.

Early in the afternoon, Sitting Bull's men withdrew, leaving nine soldiers dead and at least twenty-three wounded, likely even more with slight wounds. Crook's Indian scouts suffered one death with seven severely wounded. Sitting Bull's attackers had suffered approximately twenty fatalities.

Crook retained possession of the battlefield and therefore claimed victory. However, the next morning he led his troops back to his base camp near the Tongue River in Wyoming where he waited for reinforcements rather than venture out again after Sitting Bull. As a result, he would be far removed from where he was so sorely needed when another military force engaged Sitting Bull on June 25 at the Little Bighorn.

In fact, the battle was a major victory for Sitting Bull's men. The Sioux and Cheyenne forces had attacked when they wished, withdrawn when they wished, kept Crook from advancing toward their village, and driven Three Stars away to the south where he was of little immediate threat. Sitting Bull's warriors returned that night to sleep comfortably in their lodges, while Crook, in order to establish the appearance of victory, required his men to lie out on the dark and dangerous battlefield where they had more than met their match.

Crook was defensive about the outcome of the Battle of the Rosebud. He wrote in an official report dated September 25, well after Colonel Custer's defeat, that he had scored a major victory over a powerful force. He added, though, that had he pursued the enemy he would have met the fate that awaited Custer, thus resorting to using the deaths of Custer's men to defend his own decision to withdraw to the relative safety of his Wyoming camp. General Philip Sheridan seemed less convinced than Crook of the outcome of Crook's brief encounter on the Rosebud, writing, "The victory was barren of results, as . . . General Crook was unable to pursue the enemy . . . considering himself too weak to make any movement until additional troops reached him." [17]

BATTLE OF THE LITTLE BIGHORN

By June 24, Sitting Bull and his large following had moved into the valley of the river they called the Greasy Grass, better known to the rest of the world as the Little Bighorn. With agency Indians arriving steadily, the size of the village grew by June 25, according to conservative estimates, to over one thousand lodges and approximately seven thousand people, close to two thousand of whom were males capable of active engagement in warfare.[18] The numbers may have been even higher. White Bull thought that there were two thousand lodges and some twenty-five hundred able-bodied warriors.[19]

West of the river, the huge village spread out in six circles. The southernmost circle consisted of Sitting Bull's Hunkpapas, with 260 lodges the largest group, along with 25 lodges of Yanktonais and Dakotas. At the far north edge of the village was the circle of 120 Northern Cheyenne lodges. Between them was a combined circle of Blackfeet, Brulé, and Two Kettle tipis; and the three circles of Sans Arcs, Miniconjous, and Oglalas. Sitting Bull's tipi was positioned on the southern perimeter of his Hunkpapa cirlce, its opening facing east. His lodge was crowded: two wives, Four Robes and Seen by the Nation; his mother, Her Holy Door; his sister, Good Feather; two daughters by Snow on Her; a son by the deceased Red Woman; twin sons born three weeks earlier to Four Robes; the two stepsons that Seen by the Nation had brought with her to the marriage; and, on a temporary basis, Gray Eagle, brother of his two current wives.[20] Sitting Bull thus had many family members to care for and protect. Not surprisingly, when the soldiers attacked, Sitting Bull was deeply concerned not only with defeating the attackers but with protecting the women and children in his village.

And attack, Sitting Bull was certain, the soldiers would do, for his vision was still unfulfilled. In the evening of June 24, a Saturday, Sitting Bull removed most of his clothing, loosened his hair, and painted himself. Wearing a breechcloth and carrying a buffalo robe and his pipe, and accompanied by his nephew One Bull, he walked to a nearby ridge across from the Cheyenne circle of lodges. There, near where Colonel Custer and his Seventh Cavalry would shortly make their last stand, he prayed to Wakantanka. Sitting Bull offered the pipe to the Great Mystery and prayed for protection for his people. As additional offerings he left behind tobacco tied to sacred cherry wand sticks stuck into the ground. It is unlikely, in the ferocious battle of the next day, that any of Custer's men noticed the small, pretty sticks, or the tiny pouches of tobacco tied to them.[21]

A few days earlier, on June 21, on the Yellowstone River at the mouth of the Powder, General Alfred Terry had met aboard the supply steamer *Far West* with Colonel John Gibbon and Lieutenant Colonel George Armstrong Custer. The meeting was to finalize strategy. Custer's participation in this expedition had seemed unlikely not long before in the aftermath of his April testimony before Congress regarding graft in selling provisions at army posts. Secretary of War William Belknap had replaced the traditional army sutlers with post traders he himself appointed. The change opened the door to corruption, and the scandal touched President Grant both through his cabinet officer and his own brother, Orvil L. Grant, who took bribes in exchange for helping secure trading licenses. The testimony so angered President Grant that he ordered removal of Custer from command of the Seventh Cavalry for the upcoming expedition against the Sioux. Only Terry's direct intercession on the grounds that he needed Custer for the expedition to be successful led Grant to relent.[22]

Terry ordered Gibbon to lead his four hundred men of the Seventh Infantry and Second Cavalry west to the Bighorn River and then proceed upriver to reach the Little Bighorn valley by June 26. Gibbon's firepower was augmented by Gatling guns, a type of machine gun with a cluster of barrels that fired as the cluster rotated. Custer was to march southward up the Rosebud looking for an Indian trail that Major Marcus Reno had discovered a few days earlier. However, if the trail led westward toward the Little Bighorn, Custer was not to follow it but instead continue south on the Rosebud for another day. Then he was to turn west toward the Little Bighorn and follow it north. Terry expected that Custer and Gibbon would therefore be approaching each other on the 26th and catch the Indians between them. Terry planned to accompany Gibbon, leaving Custer in charge of the Seventh Cavalry.

Custer, from various reports, had already planned to take the initiative in pursuing Indians without being overly concerned about the precise orders. His determination to succeed personally in defeating Sitting Bull and the Sioux may have been solidified by his coming so close to missing the expedition altogether. Custer's ambitions, though, far exceeded this one encounter. According to Stanley Vestal, Custer told his Arikara scouts on June 24 that if he defeated the Sioux he would be chosen as the Grandfather, that is, the President of the United States.[23]

At noon on June 22, both the Terry-Gibbon and Custer troops departed camp below the mouth of the Rosebud. Custer's Seventh Cavalry consisted of 33 officers and 718 enlisted men, but 2 officers and 152 men had been detached between June 10 and 22, most of them to serve at the Powder River depot. That left a fighting force of 31 officers and 566 men, plus about three dozen Arikara and Crow scouts and 15 nonmilitary participants, mainly quartermaster employees. The Seventh consisted of 12 companies, each company numbering about 50, well below desired strength, with Custer's regiment overall at about sixty percent of full strength. Most troopers were armed with a Colt revolver and a single-shot

Springfield carbine. Contrary to popular depictions, not a single officer or man carried a sword of any sort. Each man carried fifty rounds for his carbine and twenty-four for his revolver with fifty additional carbine rounds in his saddlebag.[24]

By Friday, June 24, Custer was detecting fresh signs of Indians in the direction of Little Bighorn. He decided not to proceed farther south as Terry had directed but instead prepare for an attack on the village, which had grown to a size far beyond what Custer imagined. He would let his men rest the following day and attack on the 26th, permitting Terry and Gibbon to arrive from the north.

The following day, June 25, from a ridge called the Crow's Nest, Custer's scouts pointed out signs of a large village in the distance, some eighteen miles away. The bad news for Custer was that some of his troopers also reported a confrontation with Indians. Custer concluded that his presence was no longer a surprise and feared that the Sioux would flee before he could mount an attack. Accordingly, he decided to attack at once, even if both his troops and horses were tired.

By noon, Custer had his Seventh Cavalry on the move. Inexplicably, he split his command, embarking on a course of action that continues to perplex historians. He sent Captain Frederick Benteen with Companies D, H, and K southwest with the vague instructions to "move to the left, pitch into anything you come cross, and report to me." Custer later sent additional directions to Benteen telling him to move to a second set of bluffs if he saw no Indians from the first set. Subsequent orders relayed by messenger ordered Benteen, in case he saw nothing from the second set of bluffs, to proceed to the valley beyond. When Benteen could not locate a valley, and with no orders beyond the directive to hunt for the valley, he decided to turn right and try to locate Custer.[25]

Custer had also detached Captain Thomas McDougall from the Seventh Cavalry's main body, directing him to escort the pack train with Company B. The pack train followed Benteen but was well behind him.

Custer then took his remaining forces down a tributary of the Little Bighorn that would later be named Reno Creek, where he further divided his force by sending Major Reno with Companies A, G, and M to attack the village. Custer assured Reno that he would support him.

Despite that promise, Custer did not follow in support across the Little Bighorn but instead stayed to the east of the river and with Companies C, E, F, I, and L turned north. From a ridge looking northwest, Custer received his first clear view of the village. He certainly had not expected the huge assemblage that lay below him. Apparently only then realizing the enormity of the challenge, Custer sent Sergeant Daniel Kanipe to find McDougall and tell him to bring the pack train, which had all of the ammunition except what the soldiers had on their persons or in their saddlebags. Custer's sense of urgency is conveyed by his wording: "if packs get loose, don't stop to fix them, cut them off. Come quick, Big Indian camp."[26]

Custer then moved another mile north to what subsequently would be called Weir Point and once again surveyed the scene of the village. Below, Reno's men were visible forming a skirmish line. Custer summoned trumpeter John Martin and ordered him after Kanipe with a message for Benteen written out by Adjutant William Cooke: "Come on. Big Village. Be quick, Bring packs. P.S. Bring packs."[27] The packs apparently referred to the ammunition packs, which Custer certainly knew he would need, not the entire pack train, which would take longer to arrive.

Reno meanwhile had attempted to follow his orders. At approximately 3:00 P.M., he attacked but almost instantly realized that his men had no chance to survive a direct assault on the mammoth village. Reno halted the charge short of the village, where he ordered his men to dismount. They formed a skirmish line facing the Hunkpapa circle.

The attack surprised the villagers. Sitting Bull's first thoughts apparently were for his family. He mounted his mother and a sister behind him on a horse and raced to a position away from the fighting. One Bull did the same for his mother. The rest of Sitting Bull's family also made it to safety. Four Robes was so panicked that she forgot one of her infant twins and had to return for the second child. Gall's family was far less fortunate. Shots from Arikara scouts accompanying Reno killed his two wives and three children.

Sitting Bull then hurried to his tipi to get his weapons. He gave his treasured shield as well as his bow and arrows and a war club to his nephew One Bull. The nephew reciprocated by offering his Winchester repeating rife to his uncle and rode off to join the fight against Reno.

At that point, White Bull arrived at Sitting Bull's tipi. Sitting Bull had no time to prepare properly for battle. He wore no feathers and had no time to change his clothes or paint himself. Instead, he quickly mounted a black horse and rode about shouting encouragement to his warriors. Sitting Bull and White Bull, along with Four Horns, then joined the battle against Reno.

Reno and his men dropped to their stomachs to fire as the Indians attacked. Heavy fire forced the warriors back, but they quickly circled around Reno's left and attacked from the rear. Knowing that he would soon be completely surrounded, Reno ordered his men into a nearby timber. The battle continued there for about thirty minutes when Reno, recognizing that his troops were heavily outnumbered and their ammunition was running out, ordered his men to mount. He led them in a charge out of the timber and, in a race for their lives, about a mile upstream where they crossed back over the river. Some of the troopers were shot from their horses or killed as they floundered in the water. The survivors scrambled up a bluff, later to be named Reno Hill, east of Little Bighorn. There, shortly after 4:00, the badly outnumbered troopers prepared to make their desperate stand. Forty members of Reno's command were already dead. In the confusion, seventeen soldiers had not heard the order to charge out of the timber and had been left behind, although many of them later made their harried way to the bluffs.

By about 4:20, Benteen arrived at Reno Hill. An hour later, the pack train joined them, by which time the fighting around Reno Hill had sharply decreased. Major Reno and the rest of the Seventh Cavalry that had taken refuge on the bluffs still were wondering where Custer was, unaware that by the time the pack train arrived Custer and all of his men were already dead.

As Reno had recrossed the river to take refuge on the east side, Sitting Bull remained behind, leaving the pursuit to the younger men. In the clearing within the timber that Reno and his men had vacated, Sitting Bull came upon Isaiah Dorman, an African American who served Custer as an interpreter. Dorman, married to a Hunkpapa woman, was known as "Teat" to the Lakotas. He had worked as a woodcutter near Fort Rice and was viewed by Sitting Bull as a friend. Sitting Bull gave Dorman water to drink and instructed those who were moving about the dead and wounded, primarily women and boys stripping the dead and gathering anything useful, not to kill him. However, when Sitting Bull crossed the river to join the encirclement of Reno and his men, Eagle Woman, a Hunkpapa, shot Dorman to death. Others mutilated the body, a practice largely confined to individuals viewed as traitors.[28]

Another member of Custer's party who came in for similar treatment was Bloody Knife, born to a Hunkpapa father and Arikara mother and raised as a Hunkpapa before he joined his mother when she returned to the Arikaras. In December 1865, Bloody Knife had led a contingent of troops against the Hunkpapa chief Gall, resulting in Gall being severely wounded. When women found the dead Bloody Knife, who had been shot in the head, they cut off his head and carried it through the village on a pole.[29]

East of the Little Bighorn, Indians continued to hunt down straggling soldiers. Sitting Bull urged his men to leave the soldiers on the hill alone so they could return to their people and tell of the great victory by the

Lakotas and Cheyennes, but the young men especially were not yet ready to cease their attacks.

By this time, soldiers had been approaching the village from the north. These were Custer and his five companies. Turning from Reno, the Indians in overwhelming numbers converged on Custer's troops. Sitting Bull directed his warriors toward the new set of attackers and then returned to his village, riding around the Cheyenne circle of lodges to the western edge of the village where a large number of women and children had gathered. There Sitting Bull helped stand guard against a possible attack by soldiers.

Custer had divided his remaining companies into two segments, the right wing consisting of Companies C, I, and L under Captain Myles W. Keogh; and the left wing, Companies E and F, under Captain George Yates, with Custer accompanying Yates. Custer and Yates entered a large dry gulch named Medicine Tail Coulee, which headed west toward the river and the village. Apparently at this point, villagers discovered Custer's forces, drawing warriors away from Reno and almost surely saving the lives of Reno and his men. Custer did not cross the river; instead, when shots were fired across the water at him, he turned back and moved farther north. Keogh's wing seems to have stayed somewhat behind Custer and Yates to wait for Benteen and the pack train. Custer may have been looking for a way to cross the river, but if so, he never had time to find a suitable place.

Company L, under Lieutenant James Calhoun, Custer's brother-in-law, formed a skirmish line on what later came to be known as Calhoun Hill, with C and I behind in reserve. Company C tried a charge south but was forced to withdraw to Calhoun Hill, and the Lakota warriors, with Chief Gall among them, applied steady pressure to Keogh's troops. Then Crazy Horse made a daring run on horseback between Keogh's men on the hill and those in reserve. Many of the men on the hill broke ranks and fled northward, to be cut down as they raced on foot or on horseback. The men who stood and fought were quickly overwhelmed.

Custer and Yates with Companies E and F had proceeded to Cemetery Ridge in the present Custer National Cemetery. They then moved down into a basin below today's Last Stand Hill (also known as Custer Hill), and Company E dismounted. Warriors known as "suicide boys" because of their dangerous role rushed in to stampede horses, four of which usually would be held by a single trooper while his three comrades fired. Holding several horses by the reins amid the confusion and sounds of battle obviously was difficult, and it would not have been hard to spook the horses into pulling free.

Then the troopers moved up Last Stand Hill, where they were joined by perhaps two dozen survivors of Keogh's command. About forty-five soldiers charged toward the river, attempting to reach safety through some fifteen hundred warriors. They were either struck down at once or took temporary refuge in Deep Ravine, which runs to the south and west of the current Visitor Center of the Little Bighorn Battlefield National Monument, before being killed.

The remainder of Custer's men, numbering about forty-one, along with Custer himself, shot their horses and used them as breastworks. Soon they were all dead, including Lieutenant Colonel Custer and his brothers, Captain Tom Custer and younger brother Boston Custer, who had been brought along as forage master to secure food for the horses. The dead also included Custer's nineteen-year-old nephew, Armstrong Reed, who had come along for the adventure; the colonel's brother-in-law, Lieutenant Calhoun; and Mark Kellogg, a reporter for the *Bismarck Tribune*, the notes for his next newspaper article still in his pockets. According to Indian accounts, some soldiers, realizing their desperate situation, shot themselves rather than be captured. The last man fell on Last Stand Hill at approximately 4:45, about an hour after the first shots had been fired across the river at Custer's men.

Altogether, 210 men from the Custer-Yates-Keogh companies lay dead. The lone survivor on Custer's battlefield was Comanche, Captain Keogh's horse. Wounded, Comanche was transported to Fort Abraham Lincoln and nursed back to health. Retired from combat, Comanche lived the life of an honored hero, moving later with the Seventh Cavalry to Fort Riley, Kansas, finally dying during the winter of 1891–92. The total Seventh Cavalry fatalities would number 263 by the end of the battle the following day.

While Custer and his men were fighting for their lives, Reno remained on his hill four miles away with no inkling of his leader's fate, although from that hill his men could hear gunshots. Captain Thomas Weir took Company D downstream toward the firing, and Captain Benteen followed with H, K, and M. By now it was about 5:00, too late to help Custer. However, Weir got no farther than about one and one-half miles, to the high point later named Weir Point. From there, the troopers could see Indians riding around what they later learned was the Custer battlefield, sometimes shooting toward the ground. No one imagined that Custer's troops had been wiped out, and that the sporadic firing was probably to finish off some wounded soldiers. About 6:00, Indians started returning to the site of the earlier battle, and Weir and Benteen had to retreat to the hilltop where Reno had established his defense.

That night, Sitting Bull joined the warriors firing at the Reno and Benteen forces from a ridge northeast of the soldiers' position. Later that night he returned to his village.

The following morning, Monday, June 26, the battle continued but without Sitting Bull, who remained in the village until about noon, when he returned to the battle site. As he had the previous day, he urged leaving the soldiers alone. His request, though, likely would not have prevailed had Terry and Gibbon's column not been sighted coming from the north. By dusk, the village had moved, leaving just two tipis behind as burial lodges for warriors killed in the battle. Altogether, between thirty and one hundred Indians died in the Battle of Little Bighorn.

And, of course, Sitting Bull and the rest of his village left behind the bodies of the dead cavalrymen. Accounts differ regarding whether many had been mutilated. It seems most likely from firsthand accounts that most who appeared to have been mutilated actually were wounded soldiers who had then been killed with a hatchet or arrows. Much of the dispatching of the wounded fell to women. Most of the fallen troopers were stripped of their clothes. The conquerors also had helped themselves to anything else of value, including guns and bullets, some of which they captured early enough to use against Custer's men.

Not until the arrival of Terry and Gibbon in the morning of June 27 did the survivors learn what had befallen Custer and their other fellow members of the Seventh Cavalry. Writing in 1896, General Edward S. Godfrey, at Little Bighorn a lieutenant in Company K under Benteen, recalled his approach to the battlefield. Soldiers reported seeing what looked like white boulders. When Godfrey looked through his binoculars, he realized that the boulders were actually the bodies of the dead troopers, stripped of their clothes. According to Godfrey, Custer's body was not mutilated. He lay with his hands folded over his stomach, having been shot "in the front of the left temple and once in the left breast at or near the heart."[30] Stanley Vestal argued in the revised edition of his biography of Sitting Bull that White Bull had killed Custer. That claim is now largely discounted. Few if any of the Indians at Little Bighorn knew which soldier was Custer, and probably no one will ever know who killed the Seventh Cavalry leader.[31]

How much credit for the triumph over the Seventh Cavalry at Little Bighorn belongs to Sitting Bull cannot be measured precisely. Sitting Bull did not function as a commanding general directing troops during the conflict. Once Reno had launched his first bullets at the village, the die was cast. Defeat for the cavalry was all but certain given the huge numerical advantage enjoyed by the Indians.

Nonetheless, Sitting Bull had given his people the vision of a triumph over the soldiers and thus had solidified their confidence and determination. His own refusal to surrender to the United States government served as a model of resistance, and, as the greatest and most revered of the Plains Indians, he was a magnet to attract the thousands of individuals who had gathered in the village by June 25 in the valley of the Little Bighorn. Without Sitting Bull there would have been no victory. Indeed, there might not have been a battle. Sitting Bull unmistakably was the indispensable person, the pivotal maker of history during those June days.

After the battle, Sitting Bull chastised his people for having robbed the dead of their clothing and other goods, actions that violated the commands of the voice Sitting Bull had heard during his Sun Dance vision. Whether or not that disobedience was the cause, the great victory over the soldiers would be short lived.

NOTES

1. The phrase "one nation indivisible" would be immortalized in the "Pledge of Allegiance," written by Francis Bellamy in 1892, and first used in schools on October 12, 1892, after a proclamation by President Benjamin Harrison. When the "under God" phrase was inserted into the Pledge in 1954 in response to Congressional action, the addition separated the original elements of the phrase: "one Nation under God, indivisible, with liberty and justice for all." For the history of the "Pledge of Allegiance," see Richard J. Ellis, *To the Flag: The Unlikely History of the Pledge of Allegiance* (Lawrence: University of Kansas Press, 2005).

2. Quoted in Dee Brown, *The Year of the Century: 1876* (New York: Charles Scribner's Sons, 1966), 127.

3. For accounts of the Centennial Exhibition, see James D. McCabe, *The Illustrated History of the Centennial Exhibition* (Philadelphia: National Publishing Company, 1876); Giberti Bruno, *Designing the Centennial: A History of the 1876 International Exhibition in Philadelphia* (Lexington: University Press of Kentucky, 2002); and Dee Brown, *The Year of the Century: 1976.*

4. See Nicholas Lemann, *Redemption: The Last Battle of the Old Civil War* (New York: Farrar, Straus and Giroux, 2006) for Southern resistance to Reconstruction.

5. John S. Gray, *Centennial Campaign: The Sioux War of 1876* (Ft. Collins, CO: Old Army Press, 1976), 31–44.

6. The preceding material regarding the battle at Powder River is based on Gray, 47–58.

7. George Crook, *General George Crook: His Autobiography*, ed. Martin F. Schmitt (Norman: University of Oklahoma Press, 1946), 192–93.

8. Wooden Leg, *Wooden Leg: A Warrior Who Fought Custer*, interpreted by Thomas B. Marquis (1957; Lincoln: University of Nebraska Press, 1962), 171–72.

9. Gray, 324.

10. Wooden Leg, 178–79.

11. Stanley Vestal, *Sitting Bull: Champion of the Sioux*, 2nd ed. (1957; Norman: University of Oklahoma Press, 1898), 143, 145.

12. James R. Walker, *Lakota Belief and Ritual,* ed. Raymond J. DeMallie and Elaine A. Jahner (1980; Lincoln: University of Nebraska Press, 1991), 121.

13. Robert M. Utley, *The Lance and the Shield: The Life and Times of Sitting Bull* (1993; New York: Ballantine Books, 1994), 135.

14. Wooden Leg, 193–95; Utley, 135.

15. This account of Sitting Bull's visions is based on Vestal, 148–51; and Utley, 136–38.

16. See Gray, 110–24, for the detailed analysis of the Battle of the Rosebud on which this description is based.

17. Gray, 124.

18. Utley, 142.

19. Vestal, 154. For a variety of other estimates, see Gregory F. Michno, *Lakota Noon: The Indian Narrative of Custer's Defeat* (1997; Missoula, MT: Mountain Press Publishing Company, 2004), 3–20.

20. Utley, 143–44.

21. Vestal, 156–58; Utley, 144.

22. Gray, 59–71.

23. Vestal, 157.

24. Except where specifically noted, this discussion of the Battle of the Little Bighorn is synthesized from many sources, most prominently Gray, Vestal, Utley, Michno, E. A. Brininstool, *Troopers with Custer: Historic Incidents of the Battle of the Little Bighorn* (1952; Lincoln: University of Nebraska Press, 1989); Jerome A. Greene, ed. *Lakota and Cheyenne: Indian Views of the Great Sioux War, 1876–1877* (Norman: University of Oklahoma Press, 1994); David Humphreys Miller, *Custer's Fall: The Native American Side of the Story* (1957; New York: Meridian, 1992); and a helpful publication available at the National Monument: Mark L. Gardner, *Little Bighorn Battlefield National Monument* (Tucson: Western National Parks Association, 2005).

25. See "Capt. Benteen's Own Story of the Custer Fight," in Brininstool, 75–77.

26. Gray, 177.

27. Gray, 177.

28. Utley, 153.

29. Utley, 74–75, 153.

30. General E. S. Godfrey, letter to E. S. Paxson, 16 January 1896, McCracken Research Library of the Buffalo Bill Historical Center, Cody, Wyoming.

31. Vestal, Sitting Bull, 172; and Raymond J. DeMallie's Foreword to Stanley Vestal's *Warpath: The True Story of the Fighting Sioux Told in a Biography of Chief White Bull* (1934; Lincoln: University of Nebraska Press, 1984), xix-xxii.

Chapter 7

EXILE IN CANADA (1876–1881)

AFTERMATH OF LITTLE BIGHORN

Sitting Bull's Hunkpapas and their allies celebrated their great victory over the U.S. military with a victory dance four nights after the battle. Meanwhile, as word of the battle spread, President Grant, Congress, and the U.S. public demanded revenge. Sitting Bull was held responsible for Custer's defeat, and the romantic idealization of the fallen cavalry leader began. The term *massacre* was applied to the battle, incorrectly, for in fact the cavalry had attacked first, and those soldiers who died fell in combat that they had initiated, a fight between two armies, not an attack by a military force on civilians.

Wasting little time translating outrage into action, President Grant on July 22 signed a bill appropriating funds to build military posts on the Yellowstone, an action General Philip Sheridan, who commanded the Military Division of the Missouri, had strongly urged and which Commanding General William Sherman supported. The next month Congress passed, and on August 12 Grant signed, a bill restoring the number of enlisted Indian scouts to 1,000 from an earlier reduction to 300. Three days later, Grant signed a bill increasing the size of each cavalry company involved in fighting the Plains Indians to 100 men.

Also on August 15, the President approved an addendum to the annual Sioux appropriation bill prohibiting any future appropriations until the Sioux gave up all claim to their unceded lands and to the western strip of their reservation west of the 103rd meridian, the latter constituting a 40-mile stretch of land in present-day South Dakota. Grant named a seven-man commission that traveled to the Indian agencies in September and October and persuaded the chiefs, faced with an alternative of starvation, to agree to relinquish the lands. There was no attempt to follow the Fort Laramie Treaty provision that required three-fourths of males to agree to yielding any of the land.[1] Indians not on the agencies, including Sitting Bull, were expected to come in and surrender unconditionally. They would have to give up their guns and horses, without which they could not hunt buffalo and maintain their traditional way of life. They would become essentially prisoners and have to learn to provide for themselves in the white man's way, by tilling the soil.

Sitting Bull was too wise not to realize the consequences of his victory. He knew that the soldiers would come again and try to kill him or take him prisoner. He also knew that such a large force of Indians as had gathered at Little Bighorn could not stay together and hope to find sufficient food for both people and horses.

The village moved eastward seeking buffalo, part moving up the Tongue River, which flows into the Yellowstone east of Little Bighorn, the rest searching downstream. By August 1, the village had reassembled on Powder River. A few days later, the village split, with bands going in different directions after game. Sitting Bull led his Hunkpapas and some Miniconjous and Sans Arcs along the Little Missouri to Killdeer Mountain in northern Dakota Territory, where he had fought General Sully in 1864.

By early September, Hunkpapas, Oglalas, Miniconjous, and Sans Arcs had congregated near Slim Buttes in Dakota Territory. Sitting Bull was there, in mourning for a son who had died after being kicked in the head, either by a horse or mule.[2]

Captain Anson Mills, under General Crook (who, after receiving reinforcements, had taken the field again in August) and with Frank Grouard scouting, discovered a small village of Miniconjous and attacked. The inhabitants fled to bluffs overlooking the village and fired down on the soldiers, who took up positions within the village. General Crook soon appeared with his main force, and Sitting Bull arrived to join the fighting as well, shooting from the bluffs and encouraging his warriors. Among the slain were women and children. Soldiers apparently enraged over the deaths of Custer and his men scalped some of the dead.[3] The army moved out the next day, Crook taking his troops to Deadwood before ending his campaign in October at Camp Robinson in Nebraska.[4]

From Slim Buttes, Sitting Bull, with the Miniconjous and Sans Arcs who had been traveling with his Hunkpapas, turned toward the Yellowstone River. Accompanying him also was Johnny Bruguier, part Indian, who was christened "Big Leggings" by Sitting Bull's people because of the wide chaps he wore. A former interpreter at Standing Rock Agency in Dakota and wanted for murdering a man in a fight, Bruguier was fortunate to receive Sitting Bull's protection, as had Frank Grouard several years before.

As Sitting Bull crossed the Yellowstone in October, his scouts reported both buffalo and soldiers in the vicinity. There also was a wagon train passing nearby. On October 10, Lakota warriors attacked the train and shot some of the mules. The train reappeared on October 15 with about 200 soldiers under Lieutenant Colonel Elwell S. Otis and again was attacked. During the fighting, White Bull, Sitting Bull's nephew, suffered a shattered left arm from a bullet.

The following day, as the soldiers and train moved forward, a lone warrior approached with a written message that Sitting Bull had dictated to Big Leggings Bruguier:

> I want to know what you are doing traveling on this road. You scare all the buffalo away. I want to hunt on the place. I want you to turn back from here. If you don't I will fight you again. I want you to leave what you have got here, and turn back from here.
>
> I am your friend,
>
> Sitting Bull
> I mean all the rations you have got and some powder. Wish you would write as soon as you can.[5]

Long Feather, a Hunkpapa, and Bear's Face, a Blackfeet Lakota, had been sent by the commanding officer of Standing Rock Agency to try to persuade Sitting Bull to surrender. They met with Sitting Bull, who reluctantly agreed to talk with the soldiers. They then conferred with Otis to set up a meeting between him and Sitting Bull.[6] The meeting of Lakotas and Otis, according to the two intermediaries, did include Sitting Bull; although he did not surrender, the meeting secured something of a brief truce. Otis deposited a store of bread and bacon with his attackers as a goodwill gesture, and both sides withdrew.[7]

BEAR COAT MILES

Sitting Bull led his entourage to Cedar Creek north of the Yellowstone where they engaged in a buffalo hunt. The peaceful interlude was not to last long, however, as the Fifth Infantry under Colonel Nelson A. Miles was rapidly approaching.

Sitting Bull used Long Feather and Bear's Face to set up another meeting, this one with Miles. The meeting occurred on October 20, with Bruguier translating. The five-person negotiating party headed by Sitting Bull included White Bull and Sitting Bull's adopted brother, Jumping Bull.

Miles wore a fur cap and an overcoat trimmed with bear fur on the cuffs and at the collar, earning him the name "Bear Coat" from the Lakotas. Miles was generally impressed with the Hunkpapa chief, finding him physically impressive as well as deliberate and reserved in his manner, befitting the nickname the great leader had received as a child—Hunkesni, or Slow.[8] In a letter to his wife, Miles acknowledged that he could have killed Sitting Bull, but to do so when he was under a flag of truce would have violated civilized rules of behavior.[9] It was equally true as Lieutenant George Baird, who was present, observed, that given the level of tension on both sides Miles and perhaps everyone involved in the negotiations could have been killed quite easily if even a single person had inadvertently fired a weapon.[10]

The discussion broke up but resumed the next day, although to no avail. At times during the first day, the discussion had seemed to be going well. Miles offered to have some of Sitting Bull's people return with him to Tongue River, with the rest coming in after going hunting. Miles even asked to accompany Sitting Bull on the hunt.[11] The longer that Sitting Bull and Miles talked on the second day, however, the more tense the situation became. Ultimately, each was demanding irreconcilable actions from the other. Sitting Bull wanted Miles and the soldiers to quit the Yellowstone area completely, whereas Miles demanded unconditional surrender and that Sitting Bull bring his people in to the Tongue River Cantonment, a military base at the confluence of the Tongue and Yellowstone rivers that soon would be named Fort Keogh after Captain Myles Keogh, who had died with Custer at Little Bighorn. At about noon, Sitting Bull and his party rose in frustration and left the meeting. Both he and Miles returned to their men and prepared for battle.

The Battle of Cedar Creek was not long in coming. About one o'clock, Miles ordered his men forward. It proved, however, to be far different from the Battle of the Little Bighorn, although many of the soldiers had at least brief thoughts of ending up the same way as Custer's men. The engagement consisted largely of some skirmishing and Sitting Bull's men steadily pulling back with the soldiers in pursuit. Casualties were light, with one Lakota killed and two soldiers wounded.[12]

Sitting Bull moved toward the Yellowstone and then, with 30 lodges, turned northward. White Bull stayed with the Miniconjous and went in to the Cheyenne River Agency to surrender. In later years, White Bull claimed that his uncle had told him not to fight any longer, which, given the nephew's recent wound and Sitting Bull's great concern for his family members, may well have been the case.[13] The great war chief who had inspired his people to victory over Custer and who had fought valiantly to preserve the old way of life certainly understood that his coalition of resistance, so powerful just a few months previously, already was coming apart.

By the end of October, Sitting Bull and his band were at Big Dry River, 25 miles below Fort Peck, which had been constructed across the Missouri near where the Big Dry emptied into it. A larger contingent of Hunkpapas camped near the Missouri close to the fort. This group agreed to surrender, but the arrival of a boatload of soldiers frightened them sufficiently to send them rushing to Sitting Bull.

Bear Coat Miles, by now given sole responsibility for catching Sitting Bull, led his troops north from Tongue River in early November and reached Fort Peck by the middle of the month. Sitting Bull, now with about 100 lodges of Hunkpapas, had his scouts closely monitor Miles's location. As the soldiers followed the Big Dry toward the Missouri, Sitting Bull led his people eastward to the Red Water, also a tributary of the Missouri.

Seeking help in locating Sitting Bull, Miles made a deal with Big Leggings Bruguier, who, like Frank Grouard, would now betray the man who had befriended and protected him. In return for Bruguier's assistance, Miles promised to help get the murder charge against him dropped.

Because Sitting Bull was unaware of his friend's treachery, Bruguier was able to move freely about the Hunkpapa camp. On December 3, he left the camp and three days later met Lieutenant Frank D. Baldwin, who commanded three of Miles's companies. Bruguier told Baldwin where Sitting Bull was located, near the mouth of the Milk River, and formally joined the army as a scout.

Baldwin led his men toward Sitting Bull's camp but somehow bypassed it before dawn on December 7 without seeing any Hunkpapas. Jumping Bull, however, saw the soldiers and rode up close to Baldwin, who mistook him for one of the army scouts. Alerted, the Hunkpapas crossed the ice-covered Missouri to the south bank and took up positions on high ground above the river. Baldwin's men could not help thinking of Custer's Seventh Cavalry and were leery of heading into an ambush and being wiped out. They tried to follow across the ice, but when the Hunkpapas fired on the soldiers from across the river Baldwin positioned his men on a hill on the north side. A ferocious storm hit that night, and the soldiers, bitterly cold, marched back to Fort Peck.[14]

Baldwin, his men riding in wagons drawn by mule teams, caught up with Sitting Bull again on December 18 at Ash Creek, southeast of Big Dry River. Most of the Hunkpapa warriors were out hunting, but those still in camp (which included about 120 tipis) made a stand against the advancing soldiers while women and children took to the hills to escape. Several shots from a howitzer, however, sent the men retreating. There was no loss of life, but Sitting Bull lost his village and almost everything in it, including meat, blankets, several hundred buffalo robes, the tipis themselves, and a large number of horses and mules. Such a loss would have been serious anytime, but in the middle of winter it was disastrous. In addition, Baldwin enjoyed the psychological effect of a victory over the most-wanted Indian in the country. Fortunately for the Hunkpapas, they did manage to carry with them many of their weapons and much of their ammunition (which they had acquired by trading with the Slotas).[15]

Sitting Bull and at least some of his Hunkpapas probably reached Crazy Horse's village near where the Tongue River rose out of the Bighorn Mountains near the Montana-Wyoming line about January 15, 1877, although there is some uncertainty as to whether the meeting occurred.[16] If the meeting did take place, it was shortly after Crazy Horse had led some 500 to 600 Lakotas and Cheyennes against Miles at the Battle of Wolf Mountains along Tongue River on January 8. Crazy Horse almost overran the army positions before being driven back by determined resistance, low ammunition, and the onset of a blizzard. Casualties were low, but Miles claimed victory when the attackers withdrew.[17]

The arrival of Sitting Bull at Crazy Horse's village would have been the final meeting between the two great leaders. On May 6, 1877, Crazy Horse led approximately 900 of his starving followers into Camp Robinson, Nebraska, to surrender. Four months later, on September 5, the great Oglala warrior was dead. Little Big Man, who had fought beside Crazy Horse at Wolf Mountains and later became an agency policeman, helped arrest him. When they arrived at a building with barred windows, Crazy Horse tried to break away. As Little Big Man held onto one of his arms, a soldier drove his bayonet into Crazy Horse's stomach.[18] Sitting Bull was convinced that the soldiers had a similar fate in store for him.

LAND OF THE GRANDMOTHER

Sitting Bull had been considering crossing into Canada as a fall-back position if staying in the Plains became untenable, and in February he announced his intention to do just that. The pain of leaving his native land and moving across the border was eased somewhat by the Lakotas' historical association with the British and Canadians. They had been allies of the British during the French and Indian Wars, which culminated with the Treaty of Paris in 1763 and the awarding of New France, France's Canadian possessions, to Great Britain and Spain. That loyalty had persisted through the American Revolutionary War and the War of 1812. Sitting Bull still possessed the medals that his grandfather had received from King George III.[19] In addition, some of Sitting Bull's closest associates, including his cousin Black Moon, already had made that journey north. Others who would precede him into Canada included his uncle Four Horns, who arrived in March.

Sitting Bull and his by now small village of about 15 tipis crossed the Missouri River from Fort Peck, where they barely escaped with their lives from a flash flood caused by melting ice. At a council of chiefs 60 miles northwest of Fort Peck, Sitting Bull announced his intention of continuing to Canada and watching from there to see what happened to those who turned themselves in to the agencies. He was determined not to surrender his weapons and horses, and if that was forced on others he would remain north of the border. In early May 1877, Sitting Bull, whose assemblage had grown to about 135 lodges (totaling 1,000 people), crossed the *chanku wakan*, the sacred road (also known as the Medicine Line or the Big Road) into Canada.[20]

Waiting to meet Sitting Bull were the Northwest Mounted Police, who had been formed just three years earlier.[21] Especially anticipating Sitting Bull's arrival was the courageous, highly skilled, and thoroughly honorable Major James M. Walsh, commander of Fort Walsh. Inspector Walsh, known as "White Forehead" to Canadian Indians, decided to pay the new arrivals a visit. The Lakota would give him another name, "Long Lance," in response to the white-and-red pennons that adorned the lances the Mounties carried.

With six other Mounties, Walsh arrived at Sitting Bull's camp near Pinto Horse Butte at the western edge of Wood Mountains, about 60 miles inside Canada and almost directly north from Fort Peck. Although Walsh was warned by Spotted Eagle, a Sans Arc chief, that he was approaching the camp of a great chief, Walsh rode straight in, surprising the onlookers with his audacity and bravery.

Walsh rode to Sitting Bull's tipi and dismounted. He and the famous chief shook hands. Walsh made quite a striking figure: athletically built, brown curly hair, a heavy mustache, and a neatly trimmed imperial whisker (the name for a pointed beard growing from the lower lip and chin). Probably most striking, however, was the crimson coat, the origin of the nickname "redcoats" for the Mounted Police. With scout Louis Lavalie translating, Walsh explained that the new arrivals were on British soil and must obey British laws.

Walsh added that he intended to enforce the law in regard to everyone and that each person living in Canada was entitled to justice. If Sitting Bull and his people obeyed the law, the police would protect them. And, he assured Sitting Bull, there was no danger from U.S. soldiers, who were not permitted to cross the line into Canada. For the first time in many years, Sitting Bull would not have to worry about a surprise attack. At the same time, his people would not be permitted to cross the border to the United States to fight or steal and then return.

To demonstrate his sincerity and his trust in Sitting Bull, Walsh and his men spent the night in the camp. As they were preparing to leave the next day, one of Walsh's scouts, Gabriel Solomon, told him that three Assiniboines had just entered the village with stolen horses, some of them taken from a Catholic priest named Father De Corby. Knowing that Sitting Bull must understand that the law applied to everyone without exception, Walsh instructed his men to arrest White Dog and his two ac-complices. White Dog was known as a great warrior with a temperament that could easily lead him to fight back. Nonetheless, the men accosted White Dog, who responded angrily and denied the charge of horse theft. In fact, stealing horses was standard practice with the tribes as a way to replenish their herds. Walsh knew, however, that some of the old ways had to be abandoned for the sake of peace and harmony. Had Sitting Bull sided with the accused, Walsh's party could easily have been killed, but he did not intervene. Sitting Bull quickly developed respect for Walsh and truly wanted to live peacefully in the land of the Great Grandmother, as the Indians referred to Queen Victoria.[22]

And live in peace Sitting Bull generally did during his stay in Canada, but not always easily. Walsh proved a fair and sympathetic official who believed that the Lakotas had been treated badly by the U.S. government. He would be the first white man who truly functioned as an advocate for Sitting Bull.

Yet Walsh was himself limited by the position of his government to-ward Sitting Bull. Custer's destroyer was not a welcome guest. The Cana-dian government would not force Sitting Bull to leave, but it hoped that he would voluntarily accede to the U.S. demand to return and live on a reservation. To facilitate that decision, Canadian officials tried to per-suade the U.S. government to drop its demand for unconditional surren-der and permit Sitting Bull and his people to retain their horses and guns. The United States alternated between desiring Sitting Bull's return and hoping that Canada would declare Sitting Bull's people Canadian Indians and therefore assume permanent responsibility for them. The presence of Sitting Bull on Canadian soil proved a continuing irritant to diplomacy between the two countries.[23]

A number of U.S. delegations journeyed north to try to persuade Sitting Bull to accept unconditional surrender, albeit, as they inevitably argued, with good treatment awaiting him on his return. The delegations started with a visit on May 26, 1877, by a Black Robe, Abbot Martin Marty, a missionary from Standing Rock Agency in Dakota Territory, and two other men. Sitting Bull held the men prisoner while he inquired of Major Walsh what he should do about them. The course of action demonstrated both Sitting Bull's reliance, which would steadily grow, on Walsh's opinion and help as well as his desire not to do anything that would upset his new redcoat friend. Sitting Bull kept the visitors in his camp for six days until Major Walsh arrived with a delegation that included Lieutenant Colonel Acheson G. Irvine, assistant commissioner of the Mounted Police. The three were then released.[24]

Some aspects of life in Canada agreed considerably with Sitting Bull. For the moment, buffalo were plentiful, and trading was convenient and reasonably honest at Wood Mountain, where the French-Canadian trader Jean Louis Legaré quickly came to earn Sitting Bull's trust.

A U.S. commission headed by General Alfred Terry was dispatched to Canada in October 1877 to urge Sitting Bull's return. Only with great reluctance did the great war chief agree to meet Terry, the man he blamed for sending Custer to attack his village at Little Bighorn. Contributing to Sitting Bull's reluctance to meet with the commission was the recent death of his nine-year-old son by Red Woman, who had died six years earlier. The meeting understandably did not go well. Sitting Bull demonstrated his scorn for the proceedings by not starting with the standard pipe-smoking ceremony and then leveled many complaints against the United States.

The commission went away empty handed, but newspaper accounts by reporters Jerome Stillson of the *New York Herald* and Charles Diehl of the *Chicago Times* introduced Sitting Bull to the U.S. reading public for the first time as a real human being rather than a marauding savage.[25] Stillson also drew a picture of Sitting Bull. Either that sketch or one drawn at the same time by a police surgeon, Dr. Nevitt, appeared on the cover of *Harpers Weekly* on December 8, 1877, the first likeness of the Hunkpapa ever to reach a wide audience.[26]

By 1878, large numbers of additional Lakotas, including many of Crazy Horse's Oglalas, had moved north to join Sitting Bull. The approximately 800 lodges (housing 5,000 people, including 1,500 warriors) included 45 lodges inhabited by the Nez Percés, among them the war chief White Bird, who had fled successfully across the border as Colonel Miles was cornering the great Nez Percé leader Chief Joseph. Chief Joseph, after a long and heroic 1,000-mile effort to reach safety in Canada, had finally been compelled to surrender on October 5, 1877, just 30 miles short of his goal.[27]

The increased numbers worried Canadian officials, who feared hostilities between tribes from the United States and Canada. For a time, sufficient buffalo remained between Cypress Hills and Wood Mountain, but it was only a matter of time until their numbers dwindled, which created greater competition among the various Indian bands. Sitting Bull, however, held firmly to his commitments to Major Walsh. When necessity dictated going further afield for game, he generally stayed above the boundary and sent small hunting parties into Montana.

On one occasion when Sitting Bull had ventured into Montana, he found himself again doing battle with U.S. soldiers. In June 1879, General Terry ordered Miles to drive the Lakotas back across the border. On July 17, Sitting Bull and his party had enjoyed a successful buffalo hunt, and most of the men had left, leaving bout 120 people, mainly women and children, to butcher the carcasses. Some males, including Sitting Bull and Jumping Bull, remained to offer protection. A portion of Miles's force spotted the Lakotas, and Crow and Cheyenne scouts accompanying the soldiers immediately attacked.

A Crow named Magpie challenged Sitting Bull to meet in single combat. Sitting Bull, who had demonstrated his courage countless times over the years, agreed despite being in his late forties. The two men raced their horses at each other. Magpie shot first, but his gun misfired. Sitting Bull then fired, hitting Magpie in the head and killing him. Sitting Bull and his warriors then turned on the rest of the scouts, but the arrival of Miles with the remainder of his forces drove the Lakotas away, and they hastened back into Canada. Sitting Bull lost five men; among the wounded was Jumping Bull.

Miles pursued Sitting Bull, and his scouts threatened pursuit across the border. Miles, however, halted on the U.S. side, and Major Walsh convinced him of Sitting Bull's peaceful intentions. Miles then declared victory and withdrew.

"A WARRIOR I HAVE BEEN"

With the buffalo disappearing and hunger growing, Sitting Bull increasingly faced great pressure to return to the United States and surrender.

He could readily see the suffering of his people, but he also knew what surrender would mean—if not death for himself, then at least the end of the Lakota way of life and, to a great extent, the end of the Lakotas themselves.

In May 1880, Sitting Bull sent his nephew One Bull, the person in Canada closest to him, to Fort Buford in northwestern Dakota to explore the implications of surrender and the type of conditions that Sitting Bull and his people would face. One Bull was told that the same conditions still applied—surrendering of weapons and horses—but that the Lakotas would be well treated and given ample food. Sitting Bull, however, found it extremely difficult to trust many whites except for Major Walsh and the Mounted Police.

Complicating matters for Sitting Bull was the loss of his friend Walsh, who, perceived as too sympathetic to the Lakotas, was transferred to Fort Qu'Appelle, 140 miles northeast. Walsh, who had shifted earlier from Fort Walsh to Wood Mountain Post to be closer to Sitting Bull, was replaced by Inspector Lief N. F. Crozier. Crozier and Lieutenant Colonel Acheson G. Irvine, installed as commissioner in the fall, began to pressure Sitting Bull to return to the United States.

A new U.S. emissary, Edward H. "Fish" Allison, was sent by Miles to try to persuade the bands who had moved into Canada to return and surrender. He enjoyed success with many, including Gall, once a close friend of Sitting Bull's but by that time a critic of Sitting Bull and a competitor for leadership.[28] Gall's jealousy of Sitting Bull apparently was behind his charge that the great Hunkpapa leader had not been present at the Battle of Little Bighorn.[29]

By late 1880, Sitting Bull was vacillating, agreeing to return, then changing his mind. January 1881 found Sitting Bull's Hunkpapas with so little to eat that they bartered almost all of their remaining 150 buffalo robes to traders at Wood Mountain for food. Commissioner Irvine stressed that they would receive neither a reservation nor food in Canada. Still more of Sitting Bull's people gave in and headed south.

Increasingly pinched between terrible alternatives, Sitting Bull sent a delegation of his own to Fort Buford in April. One Bull once again made the journey, accompanied by Bone Club, a son of Four Horns. The delegation found those who had surrendered at Fort Buford to be reasonably content, but One Bull spoke negatively of conditions there, perhaps seeing the price paid to be well fed.

Desperate for food to feed his people, Sitting Bull in April led his camp eastward toward Willow Bunch where Jean Louis Legaré now did his trading. Sitting Bull found his friend and trading partner willing to supply food, but

Legaré also pressured him to return to the States. In fact, he offered to transport to Fort Buford in his carts both those who wished to surrender and another fact-finding delegation that could report back yet again to Sitting Bull.

Old Bull, one of Sitting Bull's representatives during the May trip, was so impressed that the soldiers had provided food, tents, and blankets that he resolved to surrender. When Old Bull returned, he found that Sitting Bull had left for Fort Qu'Appelle to confer with Major Walsh. Without waiting for Sitting Bull's return, Legaré transported another group of Lakotas to Fort Buford, including Old Bull and Many Horses, Sitting Bull's oldest daughter, who decided to use the opportunity to elope with the man she loved. When they arrived at Fort Buford, they were put aboard steamers with earlier arrivals and transported to the army post at Fort Yates, the military post at Standing Rock, below Bismarck along the Missouri.

The trip to Fort Qu'Appelle was a great disappointment for Sitting Bull, who learned that Walsh, in ill health, was in the East. Walsh, still thinking of his friend, had tried unsuccessfully to get permission to visit the President of the United States to secure guarantees of Sitting Bull's safety.[30] Canadian officials continued trying to persuade Sitting Bull to give in, with Canadian Indian Commissioner Edgar Dewdney offering to accompany him to Fort Buford to ensure good treatment. Still, Sitting Bull was uncertain.

Sitting Bull headed back to Willow Bunch on June 16. By July 12, Legaré began another trip to Fort Buford, this time with Sitting Bull accompanying him. Of the many prominent chiefs who once had ridden with Sitting Bull, only Four Horns, ever faithful to his nephew, remained by his side. Sitting Bull's followers now numbered fewer than 200. No one, however, was certain that he would not again change his mind, so a train of six wagons laden with supplies set out from the fort to meet him and his companions. On July 16, the two parties met, and the Lakotas hungrily devoured the food. In addition, Captain Walter Clifford, in a small party of seven, rode out to meet Sitting Bull and reassured the chief that his daughter, Many Horses, was fine. Clifford commented regarding Sitting Bull, with unusual perception and sympathy, that "nothing but nakedness and starvation has driven this man to submission, and that not on his own account but for the sake of his children, of whom he is very fond."[31]

As the travelers made their way south, they passed the site of an old buffalo hunt. Stretching far into the distance lay buffalo bones, skulls, and partly mummified legs. Sitting Bull surely understood the significance of the scene—how quickly the connecting thread between past, present, and future had been broken. He could well have seen himself and his way of life there among the grass and flowers growing up around the bones.[32]

On July 19, 1881, Sitting Bull and the others in his party entered the parade grounds at Fort Buford. Sitting Bull had much of his family with him: two wives, twins born in 1876 just before the battle against Custer, another set of twins born in 1880, an adolescent daughter, the two step-sons—Little Soldier and Blue Mountain—by Seen by the Nation, and One Bull and his family. Jumping Bull and Sitting Bull's brother-in-law, Gray Eagle, had arrived earlier. Many Horses, recently married, and her husband were at Standing Rock.

Sitting Bull dismounted and shook hands with Major David Brotherton, the Fort Buford commander. It is impossible to thoroughly understand how distressed Sitting Bull must have felt at that moment. Surely his ragged appearance—a thin, dirty calico shirt, black leggings, and an old blanket about his waist—reflected not only the great privation that his people had been suffering but also his deep personal despondency. Brotherton agreed to postpone the formal surrender until the next day.

On July 20, 1881, at 11:00 a.m., the man who had gathered together a mighty army and handed the U.S. military an overwhelming defeat at Little Bighorn, surrendered. Sitting Bull, his son Crow Foot beside him, sat next to Major Brotherton in the major's office. Sitting Bull laid his fine Winchester rifle on the office floor between his feet. When it came time for Sitting Bull to speak, he sat quietly for several minutes, then motioned for Crow Foot to hand the rifle to Brotherton. "I wish it to be remembered," Sitting Bull said, at least according to a *St. Paul Pioneer Press* reporter, "that I was the last man of my tribe to surrender my rifle." Stanley Vestal, however, reported that One Bull described his uncle as actually saying nothing, although the by-then elderly One Bull may simply have forgotten some of the details. Brotherton later donated the rifle to the Smithsonian Institution.[33]

Elsewhere at that time, in an ironic congruence of events, a burial detail was interring the remains of Custer's men around a new granite monument on the battlefield at Little Bighorn. The legend of Custer was growing, evidenced by still another event occurring at that moment. John Mulvaney was painting a very large canvas depicting what he called *Custer's Last Rally*.[34]

At the time, Sitting Bull appeared unable to face what the future held for him. He told Brotherton that he wished to be able to live where he chose, to hunt as he had, and to be able to visit Major Walsh and Captain Alexander Macdonell (the latter another Mountie he had come to respect). None of this, of course, would be permitted.[35] If he were psychologically in a temporary state of denial, the real world soon came rushing in on him. Not long after the surrender, Sitting Bull composed a brief, sad song:

A warrior
I have been
Now
It is all over
A hard time
I have[36]

NOTES

1. John S. Gray, *Centennial Campaign: The Sioux War of 1876* (Ft. Collins, CO: Old Army Press, 1976), 257–64.

2. Robert M. Utley, *The Lance and the Shield: The Life and Times of Sitting Bull* (1993; New York: Ballantine Books, 1994), 166; Stanley Vestal, *Sitting Bull: Champion of the Sioux*, 2nd ed. (1957; Norman: University of Oklahoma Press, 1998), 183.

3. Vestal, 187.

4. Gray, 246–51. For an extensive account of the battle, see Jerome A. Greene, *Slim Buttes: An Episode of the Great Sioux War* (Norman: University of Oklahoma Press, 1982).

5. Jerome A. Greene, *Yellowstone Command: Colonel Nelson A. Miles and the Great Sioux War, 1876–1877* (1991; Norman: University of Oklahoma Press, 2006), 88–89.

6. Greene, *Yellowstone Command*, 89.

7. Utley, 170; Greene, *Yellowstone Command*, 89–90; Jerome A. Greene, ed., *Lakota and Cheyenne: Indian Views of the Great Sioux War, 1876–1877* (Norman: University of Oklahoma Press, 1994), 98.

8. Nelson A. Miles, *Personal Recollections and Observations of General Nelson A. Miles* (Chicago: Werner, 1896), 226.

9. Greene, *Yellowstone Command*, 96.

10. George W. Baird, "General Miles's Indian Campaigns," *Century Magazine* 42 (July 1891), 351–70.

11. See Vestal, 195–98, for a transcription of part of the conversation.

12. Greene, *Yellowstone Command*, 100–05; Robert Wooster, *Nelson A. Miles and the Twilight of the Frontier Army* (1995; Lincoln: University of Nebraska Press, 1996), 84–85.

13. Vestal, 204.

14. Greene, *Yellowstone Command*, 136–38.

15. Greene, *Yellowstone Command*, 141–43; Utley, 178–79.

16. Utley, 179; Greene, *Yellowstone Command*, 153.

17. Wooster, 88–89, Greene, *Yellowstone Command*, 165–76.

18. Dee Brown, *Bury My Heart at Wounded Knee: An Indian History of the American West* (1971; New York: Bantam Books, 1972), 290–96.

19. Grant MacEwan, *Sitting Bull: The Years in Canada* (Edmonton: Hurtig Publishers, 1973), 87.

20. Utley, 182; MacEwan, 84.

21. For a history of the Royal Northwest Mounted Police during that time, see A. L. Haydon, *The Riders of the Plains: A Record of the Royal North-West Mounted Police of Canada, 1873–1910* (Toronto: Copp Clark Company, 1910).

22. See MacEwan, 85–89, for the meeting.

23. MacEwan, 104–10, discusses issues of international diplomacy raised by Sitting Bull's presence in Canada.

24. MacEwan, 100–02.

25. Utley, 194–97.

26. Utley, 373.

27. See Dee Brown, *The American West* (1994; New York: Touchstone Book, 1995), 255–64, for a succinct account of Chief Joseph's flight toward Canada. A much fuller account of Chief Joseph occurs in Kent Nerburn, *Chief Joseph and the Flight of the Nez Perce* (New York: HarperSanFrancisco, 2005).

28. Utley, 217–20, discusses Gall's agreement to surrender, resistance, and final acquiescence.

29. MacEwan, 73–74.

30. MacEwan, 184–88.

31. Utley, 230.

32. Vestal, 231.

33. Vestal, 233; John C. Ewers, "When Sitting Bull Surrendered His Winchester," in *Indian Life on the Upper Missouri* (Norman: University of Oklahoma Press, 1968), 175–81.

34. Vestal, 233.

35. Utley, 233.

36. Utley, 233; Frances Densmore, *Teton Sioux Music,* Smithsonian Institution, Bureau of American Ethnology, Bulletin 61 (Washington, D.C.: Government Printing Office, 1918), 459.

Chapter 8

RESERVATION LIFE AND SHOW BUSINESS (1881–1885)

FORT RANDALL

Sitting Bull wanted to remain at Fort Buford after his surrender until the rest of his Hunkpapas arrived from Canada. Instead, he and those who had returned with him were put aboard the steamer *General Sherman*, named after the commanding general of the military, and transported to a landing near Bismarck, North Dakota, where they arrived on July 31, 1881.

Sitting Bull's appearance when he walked down the gangplank was hardly that of a great leader. He wore blue pantaloons, an old white shirt, moccasins, and a pair of dark goggles to protect his eyes, which had been bothering him for some time.[1] Nonetheless, he was treated as a major celebrity. B. D. Vermilye, secretary to the general manager of the Northern Pacific Railway, invited Sitting Bull to ride in the manager's private railway car from the dock into town, but the war chief refused. Having never been on a train, he chose to ride with his other chiefs in an army ambulance. In Bismarck, Sitting Bull was guest at a magnificent dinner held at the Merchants Hotel. He was especially surprised at the ice cream, wondering how it could be kept frozen in warm weather.

Returning to the boat, Sitting Bull met Lulu Harmon, daughter of Matilda Galpin, also known as Eagle Woman, who had accompanied Father De Smet on his trip to talk peace with Sitting Bull back in 1868. Harmon was acting as interpreter. Sitting Bull, who had learned to write his name from Gus Hedderich, a trader, when he was in Canada, earned some money by selling his autograph to onlookers.

The *General Sherman* reached Standing Rock Reservation on August 1.[2] The reservation straddled the current states of North and South Dakota, from Cannonball River and Cedar Creek in the north to below Grand River in the south. Fort Yates, named after Captain George Yates, one of Custer's officers killed at Little Bighorn, was located near the eastern boundary in what today is North Dakota. Waiting to greet Sitting Bull was Running Antelope, one of the four Hunkpapa shirt wearers chosen in 1851; long before Sitting Bull's surrender, Running Antelope had incurred his displeasure by accepting reservation life. When the former shirt wearer went to shake hands with Sitting Bull, he noticed the Hunkpapa chief wiping away tears.

Given the possible alternatives, Sitting Bull wanted to stay at Standing Rock with his people, including his daughter Many Horses, who had returned to him after leaving her husband; however, he was forced to await an official decision regarding his ultimate destination. While waiting, he agreed to sit for a photograph by Orlando S. Goff, a photographer from Bismarck. The photograph was the first taken of Sitting Bull, who disliked the picture because he thought that it made him appear white.[3] The picture prefigured the struggle that Sitting Bull waged for the rest of his life to avoid being transformed into an imitation white man.

Then came the bad news. Sitting Bull and his fellow Canadian exiles were to be moved to Fort Randall just north of the Nebraska border. Disappointed and angered, Sitting Bull, along with the rest of his group, had to be forced onto the *Sherman* at bayonet point on September 9. When his nephew One Bull refused to board, a soldier knocked him down with a rifle butt. Sarah A. Evans, visiting at Fort Randall, heard from a family friend, a Lieutenant Ogle, that when Sitting Bull realized he had no choice but to board the *Sherman* he removed his tomahawk and knife and threw them to Ogle. The lieutenant later gave the tomahawk to Mrs. Evans.[4]

For 20 months, Sitting Bull lived separated from most of his people, hoping that the decision would be reversed. Except for the separation, however, life at Fort Randall was reasonably benign. Sitting Bull was permitted wide latitude in presiding over his small community. Stanley Vestal quotes Lieutenant Colonel George Ahern of the 25th Infantry, who was in close contact with Sitting Bull at Fort Randall, that he came "to admire him for his many fine qualities."[5]

In October 1881, Sitting Bull agreed to have his portrait painted by Rudolf Cronau, a German magazine correspondent. Cronau also painted a portrait of One Bull. At the request of Colonel George Andrews, the commander at Fort Randall, Cronau exhibited his paintings in a room at the fort. The paintings, which included some depicting residents of Standing Rock, excited great interest among the Hunkpapas at Fort Randall.[6]

During his stay at the fort, Sitting Bull returned to drawing pictographic autobiographies. The Presbyterian missionary John P. Williamson arrived with a copy of Sitting Bull's earlier autobiographical drawings, which he had created for Jumping Bull. The copy, made by Four Horns, had come into the possession of Dr. James Kimball, post surgeon at Fort Buford, and from there had been passed along to the surgeon general in Washington. Selections had been published in various periodicals, and the army wanted to know more about the drawings. Sitting Bull, however, was reluctant to talk about the pictures depicting battles with the U.S. army that was currently holding him prisoner.[7]

Sitting Bull made three more pictographic autobiographies in 1882 using pictorial techniques he learned from Cronau. Both humans and horses appear much more realistic in these new pictographs. The horses, for example, are filled out rather than the thin figures of the first series and exhibit greater variety in posture. Sitting Bull signed the new pictures with his written name rather than the image of a sitting buffalo that he used in the earlier drawings. Sitting Bull drew the three series respectively for Lieutenant Wallace Tear, the Fort Randall post trader Daniel Pratt, and Alice Quimby, daughter of Captain Horace Quimby, a Regimental Quartermaster at Fort Randall. He apparently executed the sets of pictographs in response to helpful actions by the army officers and, in the case of the Pratt set, as a business transaction. Not surprisingly, given his current situation, he concentrated on his military exploits against Indian enemies rather than government soldiers.[8]

Finally, Sitting Bull's exile ended. Strike the Ree, a Yanktonai Sioux chief, asked the Presbyterian minister John Williamson to help Sitting Bull get back to Standing Rock. The minister complied with the request and helped Strike the Ree write to Secretary of War Robert Todd Lincoln, son of Abraham Lincoln. Lincoln forwarded the letter to Secretary of the Interior Henry M. Teller, who agreed to the transfer. Sitting Bull and his fellow exiles, 172 in all, arrived at Fort Yates on Standing Rock Reservation aboard the *Behan* on May 10, 1883. Piloting the steamer was Grant Marsh, who in 1876 had been captain of the *Far West*, in which he transported Major Reno's wounded survivors of Little Bighorn to Bismarck.

STANDING ROCK: SITTING BULL'S FINAL HOME

Life at Standing Rock Reservation was vastly different from the way Sitting Bull had lived most of his life. No longer could he travel where he pleased, hunt the buffalo, or even exercise leadership as he had done on the Plains and in Canada. The agent at Standing Rock, Major James McLaughlin, was determined to carry out his government's national policy of bringing Christianity and "white civilization" to the Indian.

When Sitting Bull arrived at Standing Rock Reservation, McLaughlin was 41 years old and had been an agent for 12 years, the past two at Standing Rock. In general, McLaughlin liked Indians, but in a paternalistic way. He was married to a Dakota, which helped him learn intratribal politics and use that knowledge to play off one Native leader against another.

Sitting Bull visited McLaughlin on May 11, the day after his arrival, to express how he wished to live. He wanted to be responsible for distributing food to his Hunkpapas, decide which men would be chiefs, and otherwise function as the great chief he had long been. He also clarified what he desired for his own personal living arrangements. McLaughlin, however, was having none of it.

Here was an opportunity for the agent to demonstrate quickly and decisively who was in charge, and he wasted no time doing that. Most Euroamericans, even soldiers who had fought Sitting Bull, expressed respect for him befitting his position and accomplishments. Not so with McLaughlin. For him, Sitting Bull would be just another Indian. He would farm like everyone else, and he must start doing so immediately. McLaughlin was determined that all authority would emanate from him, to be delegated as he thought best, according to which Standing Rock residents proved most cooperative and effective in accepting the U.S. government's version of civilization.

McLaughlin quickly labeled Sitting Bull an obstructionist, a "nonprogressive." Initially, however, he did hold out at least some hope that he could bend Sitting Bull to his will. In September 1883, McLaughlin took Sitting Bull with him to Bismarck, newly named the capital of Dakota Territory, for a ceremony in conjunction with construction of a new capitol building. Sitting Bull had his first ride on a train and, as one of the official speakers, spoke graciously while sharing the stage with Dakota Governor Nehemiah G. Ordway.

McLaughlin took Sitting Bull with him again in March 1884, this time to St. Paul, Minnesota. Sitting Bull visited, among other places, the *Pioneer Press* newspaper offices, factories, a bank, a post office, and a fire department. He was delighted with the firefighters' quick response to a fire alarm and enjoyed pressing the alarm button for an encore performance. After the trip, McLaughlin wrote in an official report that he thought the trip had helped Sitting Bull to begin accepting the type of civilization he had witnessed in St. Paul and that Sitting Bull was exerting his influence "in the right direction."[9]

Although McLaughlin would soon change his mind about Sitting Bull's acceptance of modern civilization, the Hunkpapa chief tried hard to accommodate the agent while retaining as much of the Lakota way of life as possible—certainly a difficult balancing act. Sitting Bull settled into his final home in the spring of 1884 on the north bank of Grand River not far from where he had been born in what must have seemed increasingly like another world. Sitting Bull worked effectively at farming, planting oats, corn, and potatoes, and raising horses, cattle, and chickens.[10]

Despite these accommodations with McLaughlin, Sitting Bull continued to maintain the respect of most members of his Hunkpapa community. He spoke his mind to anyone he believed needed to know the truth as he saw it, including McLaughlin and prominent officials who visited Standing Rock. Unfortunately, his efforts to enlighten others did not always go well. A Senate committee headed by Senator Henry L. Dawes of Massachusetts visited the reservation in August 1883 in regard to a proposed plan to divide the large Sioux reservation into six smaller, separate reservations for different bands, with a large segment of the land turned over to non-Indian settlers.

Sitting Bull rebuked the group and reaffirmed his leadership position. The statement infuriated one of the committee members, Senator John A. Logan of Illinois, who chastised Sitting Bull in an angry and humiliating tirade, speaking to Sitting Bull as no one had ever spoken to him before. Logan had expected humility and deference from the Indians, and Sitting Bull was not inclined to present himself that way.

Among the tools that McLaughlin and other agents used to impose their will on Indians and coerce them into desired patterns of behavior were the Indian police and Indian courts, as well as schools and religion. Sitting Bull had made extensive use of akicita to keep his warriors in line, and many young males were more than willing to take on a similar role for the agent. Offenses that could lead to arrest and punishment included traditional religious practices such as the Sun Dance. Sitting Bull's death would later come at the hands of reservation police.

Sitting Bull recognized the value of children learning more about the world in which they now lived, and which he himself had come to know more about. Accordingly, he sent his stepson, Little Soldier, to an Episcopalian school while at Fort Randall, and while living on Grand River enrolled his son Crow Foot and the four other children in his household in a Congregational school. One Bull and Jumping Bull sent their children there as well.[11] Those educational decisions did not please McLaughlin, who was strongly allied with and supported by the Catholic Church.

Martin Marty, who had visited Sitting Bull in Canada and had become bishop of Dakota Territory in February 1880, worked closely with McLaughlin. One of Marty's missionaries, Father Francis M. Craft, clashed with Sitting Bull, who brought charges against Craft. No record exists of what those charges were, but Craft's biographer believes that they involved drunkenness and adultery, possibly in response to Craft's attempts to recruit young Indian girls to become nuns.[12]

Bishop Marty informed Craft, in December 1884, that he planned to visit Pope Leo XIII in Rome the following Easter and wanted to present the pontiff with two gifts: Sitting Bull's conversion to Catholicism and a buffalo robe from Sitting Bull depicting scenes from Marty's visit to him in Canada. Marty was able the next spring to deliver the robe but not the conversion.[13]

Father Craft gave crucifixes to a number of Indians, including apparently Sitting Bull, who was photographed by D. F. Barry wearing one, either the gift from Craft or, probably more likely, the earlier crucifix presented to him by his friend Father De Smet. He may have seen the crucifix as imparting some spiritual gift, or he may have worn it simply as ornamentation. Sitting Bull remained skeptical of Christianity but was not averse to borrowing bits and pieces from other religions that he might find useful.[14] That approach to religion would contribute to his later interest in the Ghost Dance and, subsequently, to his death.

McLaughlin, playing off prominent Hunkpapas against each other, did his best to minimize Sitting Bull's influence and elevate the "progressives," that is, individuals who responded positively to his directions. Gall, increasingly at odds with Sitting Bull and jealous of the respect accorded him, proved especially amenable to McLaughlin's wishes because in serving the agent he also improved his own position at the reservation. McLaughlin and Gall both denigrated Sitting Bull's role at Little Bighorn, with McLaughlin labeling him a coward in his memoirs, *My Friend the Indian*.[15]

McLaughlin's views expressed in his 1910 book seem to reflect some revising of his initial opinions. Certainly he seemed less negative about Sitting Bull after the early trips mentioned previously, but his final judgment is unrelentingly unfair and biased:

> Crafty, avaricious, mendacious, and ambitious, Sitting Bull possessed all of the faults of an Indian and none of the nobler attributes which have gone far to redeem some of his people

from their deeds of guilt. He had no single quality that would serve to draw his people to him, yet he was by far the most influential man of his nation for many years. . . . I never knew him to display a single trait that might command admiration or respect, and I knew him well in the later years of his life. But he maintained his prestige by the acuteness of his mind and his knowledge of human nature. Even his people knew him as a physical coward, but the fact did not handicap the man in dealing with his following. He had many defenders at all times, and his medicine was good down to the end.[16]

One would wonder how a man utterly lacking in admirable qualities could remain influential, maintain his prestige, and have so many defenders. The account by McLaughlin clearly expresses the animus felt by a highly authoritarian figure toward an individual he could not completely bend to his will.

As the early years of Sitting Bull's life at Standing Rock passed, disappointment, sorrow, and even tedium were all too often his lot. One of Sitting Bull's saddest moments came in 1884 when his mother, Her Holy Door, died. She had been both a link to Sitting Bull's earlier life and a constant source of wise counsel and encouragement for her son. Since the death of her husband, Her Holy Door had lived with Sitting Bull, moving with him during times of triumph and periods of suffering, including the years of increasing hunger in Canada. Only three years later, another constant in Sitting Bull's life, his beloved and always supportive uncle, Four Horns, followed into the Spirit World.

THE WORLD OF SHOW BUSINESS

Sitting Bull's interest in the wider world, as well as his desire to make money, not for himself, for he inevitably gave away most of what he earned, but to practice the important Lakota virtue of generosity, led him to join an exhibition tour in September 1884. Alvaren Allen, owner of the Merchants Hotel of St. Paul, where Sitting Bull had stayed during his trip to the city with McLauglin earlier that year, was also a showman. With McLaughlin's support, he recruited Sitting Bull and built a troupe around him called the "Sitting Bull Combination."

Accompanied by McLaughlin's wife, Mary, and son, Harry, who helped with interpretation and logistics, the group arrived in New York City, took rooms at the Grand Central Hotel, and opened at the Eden Musée, a wax museum, on September 15.[17] A tipi was erected on the stage, and Sitting Bull, advertised as the "slayer of General Custer,"[18] and other Indians, all in native attire, formed tableaus of everyday scenes. The audience was treated to lectures and given the opportunity to purchase lithographs depicting Sitting Bull and his family. Also available for purchase were revised copies of Mulvaney's *Custer's Last Rally*, often referred to as *Custer's Last Stand*, showing Sitting Bull looking down on the battle from a bluff and directing the fighting.[19] Audiences enjoyed the opportunity to see Sitting Bull, who attracted full houses for two weeks in New York. The troupe then moved to Philadelphia and other cities, completing the tour in late October.

Luther Standing Bear, a Lakota student at Carlisle School in Carlisle, Pennsylvania, attended a performance of the Sitting Bull Combination in Philadelphia and later recalled the experience in his book *My People the Sioux*. Standing Bear paid his 50 cents to enter, noted the Indian items decorating the theater, and saw Sitting Bull and three other Indian men on the stage. A man, apparently Allen, came on stage and introduced Sitting Bull as the person who had killed General Custer. Sitting Bull then spoke to the audience in his own language, which, of course, Standing Bear could understand perfectly. According to the young auditor, the chief spoke of his wish to visit the President of the United States and of the need for Lakota children to be educated. Then Allen returned to the stage, supposedly to translate what Sitting Bull had said, but instead described the Battle of Little Bighorn in largely fictitious terms. After the show had concluded, the youthful Standing Bear had an opportunity to meet Sitting Bull, who invited him back to his hotel to eat and talk.[20]

BUFFALO BILL'S WILD WEST SHOW

The next year, Sitting Bull resumed his show-business career. The former buffalo hunter and army scout turned entertainer, William F. Cody, better known as Buffalo Bill, had created a touring show called "Buffalo Bill's Wild West." By the spring of 1885, Cody was ready for the third season of his show and was anxious to add the famous Sitting Bull to his cast.

Cody had tried and failed to secure Sitting Bull's participation in 1883. This time he succeeded. First came the necessary permission from the Commissioner of Indian Affairs, John Atkins, helped along by the endorsement of General Sherman. Still, Sitting Bull was unconvinced. The final selling point may have been Annie Oakley, the sharpshooter.

The Hunkpapa chief, according to several sources, had first seen Oakley perform in St. Paul on March 19, 1884, at St. Paul's Olympic Theater. He sent her money in exchange for a photograph, but she returned the money to him. The next day, however, she visited Sitting Bull and they exchanged photographs. Sitting Bull gave her the name "Tatanya Cincila," or "Little Sure Shot," and at some point, probably during his tenure with Cody's show, made her a member of his Hunkpapas and adopted her as his daughter.[21]

John M. Burke, who functioned as Cody's business manager and press agent, worked hard to sign Sitting Bull and was said to have succeeded when he noticed the photograph of Annie Oakley in Sitting Bull's home and assured Sitting Bull that he would be working with her in the show.[22] Annie Oakley's biographer, Walter Havighurst, however, claims that Sitting Bull did not meet Oakley until he joined Cody's Wild West Show and that Cody's people created the story of prior friendship as a publicity ploy, with Oakley playing along.[23]

If Annie Oakley helped persuade Sitting Bull to join Cody, so did Burke's monetary offer. The contract called for a salary of $50 per week payable each Saturday night, along with a signing bonus of $125 plus the first two weeks of salary in advance. The contact included an addendum stipulating that Sitting Bull would retain the proceeds from selling his autograph and picture.[24]

Sitting Bull joined Buffalo Bill's Wild West Show in Buffalo, New York, on June 12, 1885, and concluded his performances four months later when the show's season ended. Cody was careful to show respect to Sitting Bull and not overly sensationalize the war chief. Unlike Alvaren Allen, Cody did not introduce him as the slayer of Custer. Except for Cody himself, Sitting Bull received top billing in the show and was advertised in print with such expressions as "The Renowned Sioux Chief."[25]

Sitting Bull appeared as himself and rode in street parades and arena processionals but did not appear in mock battles. When not actively participating in the show, he was available in his tipi on show grounds to sign autographs.[26] His special position in the show as well as in history was acknowledged in various ways. During a performance at an Ohio fairground, for example, Sitting Bull was invited after the opening processional to view the rest of the show with other dignitaries from the reviewing stand.[27]

On June 22, the Wild West Show arrived in Washington, D.C., for a three-day run. Accompanied by Cody, Sitting Bull visited President Grover Cleveland. He brought along a letter that a circus staff member had written out for him and that expressed his wishes for his people. Sitting Bull then visited General Philip Sheridan, commander of the U.S. Army, at army headquarters. Neither the visit nor the letter, however, evoked a positive response from the President.[28]

On the whole, Sitting Bull was well received during his tour with Cody. That was especially true when the show visited Canada, where he was treated as a hero. He was given a ride on a St. Lawrence steamer at Montreal, and his photographs proved so popular that they sold out. To replenish the supply, Sitting Bull posed with Buffalo Bill for a portrait that often was printed with the caption "Enemies in '76, Friends in '85."

Always thinking of the welfare of his people, he asked Nate Salsbury, Cody's partner, to write to Indian Affairs Commissioner John Atkins requesting certain changes. Sitting Bull wanted Army troops to stop trespassing on reservation hay and timber lands, additional traders to be licensed to trade with the Lakotas, and agricultural instructors to be hired that spoke his people's language—all practical suggestions—but again Sitting Bull's requests were ignored.[29]

Along with Cody and Annie Oakley, Salsbury earned the respect and friendship of Sitting Bull, who adopted him as something of an honorary son at a barbecue in Boston, naming Salsbury Little White Chief. Sitting Bull also gave him an eagle feather from his headdress and a pipe.[30] Bostonians especially took to Sitting Bull, and the Hunkpapa chief was lionized in the city's newspapers. Sitting Bull's reception in the United States had initially been less generous than it was in Canada, but his popularity increased during his four months with the show. The turning point appeared to be the Boston run, which came shortly before the Canadian leg of the tour. A reporter for the *Boston Transcript* even praised Sitting Bull's dignified visage, likening his appearance to the famous Massachusetts politician and orator Daniel Webster.[31]

One of Sitting Bull's most dangerous moments during the tour came in Pittsburgh. Sitting Bull enjoyed watching the roustabouts driving tent pegs with their sledgehammers and even occasionally took a swing himself at the pegs. When the brother of a soldier killed at Little Bighorn appeared determined to avenge his brother's death. Sitting Bull, who was exercising his newfound talent with the sledgehammer, used it to knock out several of his assailant's teeth.[32]

As the season neared its end, Sitting Bull increasingly felt homesick. He readily confided in reporters that he was tired of the crowds and noise and wanted to be back in his own home. Although he had earlier expressed pleasure in traveling and learning, he was not enthralled overall with the lifestyle he had observed during the tour.

Cody, however, was pleased with the way the tour had gone. Buffalo Bill's Wild West Show had played to more than a million spectators in approximately 40 cities, turning a profit of $100,000.[33] Much of the credit for the successful season certainly belonged to the two new stars of the show, Annie Oakley and Sitting Bull. In appreciation, Cody gave his Hunkpapa star two presents: a gray horse that Sitting Bull had ridden in the show and a large white sombrero. The horse was trained to perform circus tricks; a few years later, in a grotesque echo of happier days, the horse was said to have suddenly begun going through its old routine during the turmoil surrounding Sitting Bull's death.

Not surprisingly, Cody wished to sign Sitting Bull for future seasons, but that did not prove possible. Standing Rock agent James McLaughlin hoped that Sitting Bull would be so favorably impressed with the outside world that he would return happy to adopt the new ways. Instead, Sitting Bull returned just as independent as ever and with a view of the Euroamerican world that was both perceptive and critical.

In a letter to Nate Salsbury, McLaughlin complained that Sitting Bull had not benefited from his experience and that he had squandered all of the money he earned.[34] In fact, Sitting Bull did give away much of his earnings, especially to street urchins and others in need. Dispensing money, rather than being irresponsible, was a manifestation of the virtue of generosity that characterized Sitting Bull throughout his life. Fidelity to traditional Hunkpapa virtues was important to Sitting Bull. It gave his life meaning, and it would help lead, ultimately, to his death.

NOTES

1. Robert M. Utley, *The Lance and the Shield: The Life and Times of Sitting Bull* (1993; New York: Ballantine Books, 1994), 236.

2. For a history of Standing Rock Reservation filled with informative photographs, see Donovan Arleigh Sprague, *Standing Rock Sioux*, in the Images of America series (Chicago: Arcadia Publishing, 2004).

3. Utley, *The Lance and the Shield*, 240.

4. Written statement by Sarah A. Evans in the McCracken Research Library at the Buffalo Bill Historical Center, Cody, Wyoming.

5. Stanley Vestal, *Sitting Bull: Champion of the Sioux*, 2nd ed. (1957; Norman: University of Oklahoma Press, 1998), 237.

6. Rudolf Cronau, "My Visit among the Hostile Dakota Indians and How They Became My Friends," *South Dakota Historical Collections* 22 (1946): 410–25.

7. The first pictographic autobiography, known as *The Kimball Pictographic Record*, appears in *Three Pictographic Autobiographies of Sitting Bull*, edited by M. W. Stirling (Washington, D.C.: Smithsonian Institution, 1938).

8. The Tear and Pratt records, known as *The Smith Pictographic Record* and *The Pettinger Pictographic Record*, also appear in *Three Pictographic Autobiographies of Sitting Bull*. The series drawn for Alice Quimby has been published separately as *A New Pictographic Autobiography of Sitting Bull*, edited by Alexis A. Praus (Washington, D.C.: Smithsonian Institution, 1955).

9. Utley, *The Lance and the Shield*, 260–62.

10. For details of reservation life, see Chapter 8, "The Reservation, 1880–1890," in Robert M. Utley, *The Indian Frontier of the American West, 1846–1890* (Albuquerque: University of New Mexico Press, 1984), 227–52.

11. Utley, *The Lance and the Shield*, 244, 255.

12. Thomas W. Foley, *Father Francis M. Craft: Missionary to the Sioux* (Lincoln: University of Nebraska Press, 2002), 28–29.

13. Foley, 34–35.

14. Foley, 35–38.

15. James McLaughlin, *My Friend the Indian* (Boston: Houghton Mifflin, 1910), 141, 182.

16. McLaughlin, 180.

17. Utley, *The Lance and the Shield*, 262–64.

18. Vestal, 250.

19. Gary C. Anderson, *Sitting Bull and the Paradox of Lakota Nationhood* (New York: Pearson Longman, 2007), 157–58.

20. Luther Standing Bear, *My People the Sioux* (1928; Lincoln: University of Nebraska Press, 1975),184–87.

21. Louis S. Warren, *Buffalo Bill's America: William Cody and the Wild West Show* (New York: Alfred A. Knopf, 2005), 253; Robert A. Carter, *Buffalo Bill Cody: The Man Behind the Legend* (New York: John Wiley and Sons, 2000), 274; Larry McMurtry, *The Colonel and Little Missie: Buffalo Bill, Annie Oakley, and the Beginnings of Superstardom in America* (New York: Simon and Schuster, 2005), 136.

22. Warren, 253; Carter, 282.

23. Walter Havighurst, *Annie Oakley of the Wild West* (New York: Macmillan, 1954), 52.

24. I am indebted to the McCracken Research Library for a copy of the contract.

25. Louis Pfaller, "Enemies in '76, Friends in '85—Sitting Bull and Buffalo Bill," *Prologue, the Journal of the National Archives*, 1.2 (1969): 16–31.

26. Letter from Paul Fees, Senior Curator of the McCracken Research Library, to Robert M. Utley, 28 April 1992; copy of the letter courtesy of the McCracken Research Library.

27. Clipping from the *Ohio State Journal* in the collection of the McCracken Research Library.

28. The letter is published in Pfaller, 24–25. The original is in the National Archives.

29. Pfaller, 23–26.

30. Havighurst, 57–58.

31. Pfaller, 23.

32. Annie Fern Swartout, *Missie, An Historical Biography of Annie Oakley* (Blanchester, OH: Brown Publishing Company, 1947), 93.

33. Carter, 288.

34. Pfaller, 27.

Chapter 9

RETURN TO THE SPIRIT WORLD (1886–1890)

THE LAND

The death of Sitting Bull was precipitated by several intertwining factors: his faithfulness to the traditional Lakota way of life, intertribal politics, power struggles involving reservation agents, and the perceived threat of the Ghost Dance. "I would rather die an Indian than live a white man," Sitting Bull confided to Mary Collins, a Congregationalist missionary, and he lived and died doing his best to remain an Indian.[1]

A series of actions by the U.S. government threatened to erode both the expanse of land allotted to the Lakotas and, at the same time, even more of their way of life. The pivotal issue of Sitting Bull's final years, at least from his perspective, thus became how to retain what land remained to his people, namely the Great Sioux Reservation, and the communal manner of living that his ancestors had enjoyed.

While the government was trying to persuade reservation Indians to accept individual allotments of land and abandon the collective approach to land traditionally taken by most tribes, Sitting Bull paid a visit to his old enemies, the Crows. In the fall of 1886, Sitting Bull visited the Crow Reservation in Montana, where he spent two weeks feasting and talking with his Crow hosts. Nearby stood the hill on which Custer and his men, just 10 years before, had died, and on which a large Seventh Cavalry Memorial had been erected in 1881.[2]

The meeting cemented the peace between Lakotas and Crows. The most pressing issue discussed was not old hostilities but the land question. Just a short decade ago, Sitting Bull had led perhaps the most impressive

American Indian military force in history and had subjected the might of the United States to a stunning defeat. So muchhad changed for Sitting Bull, however: exile in Canada, life on a reservation, travels during which he had witnessed the immensity of this nation that had struggled so hard to capture him, and now one more great struggle to hold onto even the reservation land and live on it as Sitting Bull believed Wakantanka had intended him to live.

Sitting Bull strongly urged his hosts not to accept individual allotments. Encouraged by the force of their old enemy's argument, the Crows agreed to resist, although for the Crows as for the Lakotas, it would be a temporary and ultimately failed resistance.

Sitting Bull received 30 ponies from the Crows, a great gift at a time when horses had become scarce for the Lakotas, once considered the greatest horsemen of the Plains. The gift, ironically, would have at least some small bearing on his death four years later. Returning to Standing Rock, Sitting Bull gave his ponies as gifts, as chiefs had given gifts for generations. Bull Head took a special liking to a black-and-white-spotted pony that Sitting Bull intended for Catch the Bear. Sitting Bull insisted that Catch the Bear have it and presented a different pony to Bull Head. The dispute over the pony contributed to lasting animosity between the two recipients, who would both die in the same violent clash that took Sitting Bull's life.[3]

Allotment in severalty, that is, separate and individual ownership, had previously been part of a number of treaties. The General Allotment Act of 1887 sought to apply the concept to all Indians, allowing 160 acres to each head of a household and lesser amounts of land to others.[4] The United States would hold the land in trust, in effect retaining title to the land, for 25 years, after which the Indian-farmer would own the land outright. Along with the allotment went citizenship. After the allotments were made, the remaining land would be acquired from the Indians and opened for settlement. The Great Sioux Reservation was particularly desirable, as it contained a large tract of land that thus could be opened to the growing population of the Dakotas.

The Sioux Act of 1888 applied the approach of the General Allotment Act specifically to the Great Sioux Reservation but reversed the chronology of the provisions, beginning with negotiations for surplus lands before apportioning individual allotments. In addition, the reservation would be divided into six smaller reservations, with the Standing Rock, Cheyenne, Lower Brulé, Crow Creek, Pine Ridge, and Rosebud Reservations home to specific Lakota bands. Nine million acres would be opened for settlement, earning the Lakota residents just 50 cents per acre. Under the Treaty of

1868, however, three-fourths of Indian males residing on the reservation would have to approve the land sale before it could occur.

Few Lakotas liked the idea of selling such a large portion of the reservation. For a people accustomed to traveling freely over the Great Plains in search of buffalo, other game, water, and sweet grass for their horses, the idea that they now had more land than they needed was incomprehensible. No one opposed the plan more than did Sitting Bull.

In these reservation years Sitting Bull, despite the obstructionist claims made against him by Standing Rock agent James McLaughlin, lived a generally quiet, peaceful, and, in most respects, cooperative life. He farmed and tended to his family. His children included two sets of twins, one born before the Battle of Little Bighorn, the other during the Canadian years. One of the earlier pair of twins, Crow Foot, had been with his father during his surrender and would die with him within a few years. An especially beloved daughter, Standing Holy, was born in 1878, and during the reservation years, his two wives gave him two more children, a boy and a girl. With so many people to care for, Sitting Bull was decidedly not a troublemaker.

Yet Sitting Bull could not countenance yielding the land. When a commission headed by Richard Henry Pratt, founder of the Indian school at Carlisle, Pennsylvania, arrived to gain the approval of reservation males in accord with the Sioux Act, Sitting Bull worked effectively behind the scenes to shore up opposition. For a month, from July 23, 1888, until August 21, the commission stubbornly persisted at Standing Rock Agency until finally accepting defeat and leaving. Pratt recommended moving ahead without Indian approval, but that proved politically unacceptable to too many political leaders back East.

Instead, 61 chiefs, including Sitting Bull, were invited to Washington, D.C. to meet with government officials. The delegation arrived on the night of October 12. On October 15, the chiefs met at the Interior Department to discuss a plan that now included a price of $1 per acre for the land released to settlement. By October 19, Sitting Bull and 46 other chiefs had agreed to accept $1.25 per acre, a counterproposal rejected by Secretary of the Interior William Vilas. After meeting with President Benjamin Harrison, who had been elected in 1888, the delegation returned home.

More legislation, however, was forthcoming. The Omnibus Bill of 1889 granted statehood to Washington, Montana, North Dakota, and South Dakota, putting even greater pressure on government officials to open up the Great Sioux Reservation for homesteading. Another Sioux Act in the same year proposed a sale price of $1.25 per acre for three years, the price to be reduced gradually to 75 and then 50 cents. A new Sioux Commission was convened to try once again to sell the redistricting plan to the Lakotas. The commission, chaired by former Ohio Governor Charles Foster, included William Warner, elected to the position of national commander of the Grand Army of the Republic in 1888; and most important, Major General George Crook, the veteran Indian fighter known to his Indian adversaries as Three Stars. Crook was a wise choice. Although he had fought against the people he must now convince, he enjoyed their grudging respect as a warrior and as a man they generally believed to be truthful.[5]

Crook put his knowledge to effective use. The commission, recognizing the difficulty of succeeding at Standing Rock because of Sitting Bull's influence, left that agency to last. Carefully and patiently, Crook explained the plan to his listeners, and James McLaughlin lobbied individuals he had previously found receptive to his directives, such as John Grass and Gall.[6] As Crook and McLaughlin's efforts were about to yield their desired effect, Sitting Bull, on August 3, led a contingent of 20 Silent Eaters on horseback into the crowd of men lined up to sign the agreement; however, Indian police led by Lieutenant Bull Head forced them back.

Soon after the requisite number of men signed, surpassing the two-thirds requirement, the Lakotas felt thoroughly betrayed once again. Just two weeks after agreeing to the land allotment, they learned that their beef rations were being reduced, the result of a budget cut mandated by Congress.[7] The two actions had nothing to do with each other, but it seemed as if they did to the people who now were faced with both the loss of their collective land and reduced rations.

Crook had made a number of promises during his discussions with the Lakotas, probably sincerely, but they were promises to promote certain policy changes that would benefit the Lakotas rather than guarantees of change. Crook assured his listeners, for example, that he would support allocating more money for education, employing additional Indians at the agencies, removing the ban on ritual dances, and compensating owners for confiscated ponies. The Indian Office invited a delegation of chiefs to visit Washington once again to follow up on these promises. This time Sitting Bull was left behind.

A new Secretary of the Interior, John W. Noble, moved to implement changes that fell within his authority, such as those involving employment and dances. General Crook's death on March 21, 1890, however, further discouraged the signers, who understood they had lost an individual who, they believed, would at least try to keep his word.

At the time, not much was going right for Sitting Bull and the Lakotas. Crops on the reservation were poor in 1889, and a drought the next year reduced the harvest even more. In 1888, blackleg afflicted the Indians' cattle, and then came the reduction in beef rations in 1889. Epidemics of measles, whooping cough, and grippe (later known as influenza) struck down many reservation residents in 1889 and 1890. Complicating conditions was the unusually harsh winter of 1889–90.

At the six agencies, the Lakota bands desperately needed help. If the help would not come from the U.S. government, and could not emanate from the Lakotas themselves, perhaps Wakantanka might intervene. A new religion that had arisen in Nevada seemed to offer hope that perhaps their great misery might be lifted.

THE GHOST DANCE

A Paiute named Wovoka, also known as Jack Wilson, began having revelations sometime during the 1880s. He believed that on one occasion he had fallen asleep during a solar eclipse and been taken up into the spirit world. He was told to return to his people and tell them that they must love each other, put aside war, live peacefully with everyone, and neither lie nor steal. If they lived this way, Wovoka said, they would be reunited with those who had died and live forever free of sickness and death. Wovoka also carried back with him instructions to perform a dance that would help bring about this great transformation.

The news of Wovoka's vision spread rapidly. For many tribes, including the Lakotas, Wovoka seemed to be a Messiah promising hope. To many people, the vision resembled the prophesied Second Coming of Christ at the end of the world. Wovoka denied seeing himself as Christ, although a Cheyenne named Porcupine asserted that Wovoka had claimed both to be Christ and to have the marks of the crucifixion on his body. Others saw similarities to the Mormons' anticipated arrival of a Messiah. Indians, especially Lakotas, increasingly interpreted the vision as a promised restoration of their past way of life.[8]

Two delegations of Lakotas traveled west in 1889 and 1890 to meet this new Messiah and ascertain the reliability of his vision. The visitors were impressed, with Short Bull, a Brulé medicine man, and Kicking Bear, a Miniconjou, quickly becoming the leading Lakota proponents of this new religion. The Lakotas especially adapted Wovoka's lessons to their own situation. Wovoka's directives were rigidly moral and completely peaceful. He taught his own Paiutes to live in harmony with both Indians and non-Indians, an inclusiveness easier for him than for the Lakotas, who felt a much higher level of resentment and greater sense of betrayal toward the United States than did Wovoka.

By the time the Lakotas first performed Wovoka's dance, at Pine Ridge in the spring of 1890, it had taken on new connotations. Given its association with the spirit world and the dead, the heavily ritualistic dance was referred to as the Ghost Dance. The Lakotas saw the dance as an act of regeneration of their people and the land, with the return of their dead relatives and friends along with the return of buffalo and other game. They also performed the dance as an act against their conquerors, who would be covered over by the new earth, in essence returning the world to what it had been before the coming of the Euroamericans.

There is little evidence to indicate that the Lakotas saw this regeneration as requiring any overt act of war on their part. James McLaughlin clearly did not see any great threat of violence in the Ghost Dance. Nor did the commander of Fort Yates, Lieutenant Colonel William Drum. Less knowledgeable individuals, however, including some of the settlers in the area and the inexperienced Pine Ridge agent, Daniel F. Royer, who regularly dashed off worrisome complaints to his superiors, were not so sure. Knowing how some people might react to the Ghost Dance, and highly suspicious of the United States military, Lakotas added an ingredient to the dance that Wovoka, committed to peaceful action, never proposed—the Ghost Shirt. This shirt, or dress for women, usually was made of white cloth (given the scarcity of buckskin) and covered with sacred symbols such as the sun and moon. Its purpose was protective. Wearers were told that the shirt would protect them from bullets. As such, the Ghost Shirt was primarily a defensive garment. Other tribes, such as the Arapaho and Cheyene, rejected the shirt as inconsistent with a peaceful ritual.[9]

Before the dance, men would fast and purify themselves in the sweat lodge. The dancers, who included men, women, and children, held hands and moved in a circle from right to left, facing a prayer tree that was planted in the middle of the circle. The dance was physically tiring, and as it proceeded the pace quickened. Physical exhaustion coupled with the high emotional level of the participants induced something akin to a hypnotic state in some of the dancers. It was not unusual for a dancer to fall to the ground unconscious and, coming to, claim to have traveled into the spirit world and seen departed loved ones.[10]

For many Lakotas, the Ghost Dance quickly filled the vacuum created by the absence of the outlawed Sun Dance. They danced as if the Ghost Dance were their final opportunity to regain their freedom and way of life. Despair bred hope, and that hope precipitated certainty in many. The dance would work, and if soldiers attacked, the Ghost Shirt would protect them. The projected date for the return of their old world, spring of 1891, provided added motivation, for the end of their suffering was almost at hand.

How much of this Sitting Bull truly believed is impossible to say. He supported the Ghost Dance at his Grand River settlement, where dances under his sponsorship were conducted enthusiastically beginning in the fall of 1890, although he himself never danced. According to Stanley Vestal, Sitting Bull admitted that he did not believe in the coming of a Messiah,[11] and he likely had seen too much of the outside world to believe that a dance could truly wipe it out. Still, Sitting Bull was a highly spiritual visionary who had trusted dreams and visions during his whole life. Perhaps he could not bring himself to reject the possibility of there being something true in this new religion. Sitting Bull was eclectic in his religious beliefs, willing to accept pieces of any faith if those pieces proved helpful. If he did not believe this new vision in its entirety, he may yet have imagined that some element of change could be achieved through it. If nothing else, the dance gave his people hope, and so long as there was hope, they might not give way utterly to despair and acceptance of the conqueror's plan for them. Whatever Sitting Bull's motivation, he must have seen some benefit to the Ghost Dance or he would not have encouraged and defended it.[12]

And defend the Ghost Dance he did. Agent McLaughlin, accompanied by his interpreter, Louis Primeau, visited Sitting Bull on November 17, 1890. A Ghost Dance was underway, and McLaughlin watched it for a time, then withdrew to spend the night with a trusted tribal policeman, Lieutenant Bull Head. McLaughlin returned the next day to try to persuade Sitting Bull to abandon the dance. McLaughlin had no significant worries about a return on the chief's part to warfare, but he knew that as long as the dance craze continued, its adherents would resist the new, "civilized" way of life toward which McLaughlin was pushing them. Sitting Bull listened politely and suggested a compromise. He and McLaughlin would travel on a fact-finding expedition westward to interview those who had seen the Messiah. If no one could show them a credible Messiah, Sitting Bull would tell his people that the religion was false. Perhaps McLaughlin should have accepted Sitting Bull's offer, but he did not. Finally, Sitting Bull followed his usual method when confronted with directives he did not like. He replied that he would have to think about what McLaughlin said, consult others, and come to see McLaughlin later, thus avoiding a confrontational rejection at that moment and allowing time for his opponent's ardor on the subject to cool.[13]

Knowing that he might be arrested if he went to the agency, Sitting Bull sent a substitute the next Saturday, November 22, to collect his rations. Others did the same, but McLaughlin refused to release the rations; henceforth, the head of the family must come in person. The new policy was aimed principally at Sitting Bull, whom McLaughlin wanted close at hand so that he could arrest him, a step that McLaughlin had been arguing for in communications with the Commissioner of Indian Affairs.

There was, of course, no just cause for his arrest, no violation of law or act of violence toward any of the military figures or civilians at Standing Rock. Being obstructionist, however, was reason enough for McLaughlin, especially in a person possessing the influence that Sitting Bull had. With Sitting Bull out of the way, arrested, and transferred to a prison somewhere else, McLaughlin could push his plans for the Lakotas more effectively and with much less opposition.

MARY COLLINS AND CATHERINE WELDON

Others also were urging Sitting Bull to reject the Ghost Dance. They included two unlikely friends of Sitting Bull's, Mary Collins and Catherine Weldon. Mary Collins, a Congregationalist missionary, arrived at Standing Rock Reservation in 1885, bringing with her some skill in nursing that apparently led to her acceptance by Sitting Bull, according to Collins, as a "medicine woman."[14] Sitting Bull also welcomed her ability to teach Hunkpapas to read, which she willingly did, but he resisted her efforts to convert him to orthodox Christianity. Collins took pride in the name that the Lakotas gave her, "Wenonah," which she interpreted as princess.

Collins and Sitting Bull established an easy relationship, referring to each other as "brother" and "sister." She felt comfortable enough with Sitting Bull to take him to task for attempting to smoke his pipe in her home, apparently missing the spiritual dimension of the pipe. She acknowledged his positive qualities: "so tender, gracious and invariably sweet,"[15] and recognized his ability to read natural signs. Collins recalled Sitting Bull's prediction of a mild 1890–91 winter, which meant that the Ghost Dance could continue being performed.

Collins tried hard to dissuade Sitting Bull from supporting the Ghost Dance, which conflicted sharply, at least in Collins's mind, with Christianity. On one occasion in early December, she participated in a religious service near Sitting Bull's settlement during a dance, hoping that the singing of "Nearer My God to Thee" might overwhelm the sounds of the Ghost Dance. When that did not work, she sought admittance to Sitting Bull's home and again attempted to convince him of the error of his ways. To demonstrate the falsity of the dance, she marched up to a man named Louis who supposedly had collapsed during the dance and lay unconscious. She demanded that Louis get up and stop faking. According to Collins, Louis sheepishly arose and slunk off.

This attempt to stop the Ghost Dance was the last time that Collins saw Sitting Bull. Her recollections of Sitting Bull are somewhat condescending but certainly demonstrate considerable fondness toward him.

Catherine Weldon was quite different from Collins. By her own admission not much of a Christian, Weldon came to Standing Rock as a member of the National Indian Defense Association. She appeared in 1888 and again in each of the next two years. Her initial effort was to urge opposition to General Crook and the rest of his commission. By 1890, she had determined to engage fully in the life of the Lakotas, even moving in with Sitting Bull along with her son, Christie, to assist with secretarial and housekeeping duties.

Gossip circulated widely in newspapers and by word of mouth that she had become Sitting Bull's wife. Her biographer, Eileen Pollack, does not believe that the two had a romantic or sexual relationship, and that Weldon got along well with Sitting Bull's two wives. At the same time, she believes that Sitting Bull may well have suggested marriage. A note written by Weldon and found in Sitting Bull's cabin after his death seems to suggest an indignant response to such a proposal: "You had no business to tell me of Chaska. Is that the Reward for so many years of faithful friendship which I have proved to you?"[16]

The reference to Chaska, who had married a white woman, would seem to imply an analogy that Sitting Bull could have drawn to a union between Weldon and himself. If so, the widowed Weldon, for all her desire to assist Sitting Bull and the close intimacy of sharing a cabin with him, appears to have found the idea of marrying him offensive. Whether that was because he was already married or an Indian or somebody she had earlier likened to a father, as she had referred to him in a letter to McLaughlin, is open to conjecture.[17]

Weldon assisted Sitting Bull financially, gave him gifts, painted his portrait, and read to him about other warriors such as Napoleon and Alexander the Great. The reading must have been rather halting, as Weldon did not master Sitting Bull's language. Perhaps Sitting Bull's son Crow Foot, who did know English, helped.[18]

Like Collins, Weldon strongly opposed the Ghost Dance, which she considered nonsense unworthy of Sitting Bull but also potentially dangerous to him, and even offered to debate Kicking Bear regarding the veracity of the dance, a challenge that Kicking Bear did not accept. She understood that McLaughlin could use the Ghost Dance as an excuse to remove Sitting Bull from the reservation. She also feared that the Ghost Dance was a Mormon invention designed to correspond to the Mormon prophecy of a Messiah and to use Indians to advance their own status in the country.[19] The Mormons at that time faced a great deal of suspicion, primarily arising from ignorance of their tenets and bias toward their religion.[20]

Discouraged by her inability to lead Sitting Bull away from the Ghost Dance, Catherine Weldon decided to leave, although apparently with the intention of returning at some point. Sitting Bull drove her by wagon to Fort Yates on October 22. In November she and her son left the area aboard the steamer *Abner O'Neal* down the Missouri River. Her destination was Kansas City. Before leaving, Christie had stepped on a nail, and during the trip he became desperately ill from lockjaw, an illness now more commonly known as tetanus. The boat ran aground near Pierre, South Dakota. After it was freed and could dock at Pierre, Weldon left the boat to seek medical help at a hospital that had been opened a year previously by five nuns, but in the middle of November Christie died.[21] Most accounts have given the son's age as about 14, but he actually was younger, having been born in 1878. Weldon herself gave the older age, likely to avoid criticism for taking someone so young to live among the Lakotas.[22]

Weldon wrote to Sitting Bull after she arrived at Kansas City, reporting her son's suffering, death, and burial, the last occurring on November 17. "Remember my boy!" she pleaded, referring to Christie as "the only son of your best friend." She further implored Sitting Bull, "And if your prayers to the Great Spirit are heard, pray to him to give me a speedy death, that my heart may find peace." Weldon signed her letter *Toka heya mani win*, Woman Walking Ahead, the name the Hunkpapas had conferred on her.[23]

Three days later, Weldon wrote again to Sitting Bull, and, a week later, sent a final letter. In these letters, she wishes that her son had died in the Dakotas and is distraught over newspaper articles that denounced her relationship with the Indians and even blamed her for causing the Ghost Dance. She also laments the necessity of leaving her trunks and most of her possessions onboard the steamer and complains that she has not received them yet. There is no record of her ever reclaiming the trunks. The letters beg Sitting Bull to write back to her and demonstrate clearly that she still considered Sitting Bull a friend, perhaps the only friend in whom she could confide her deepest feelings.

Sitting Bull received her letters but did not answer them. In fact, he had little time left himself, and while he would have shared Weldon's sorrow over her son's death, he had his own people's welfare to consider.[24] Weldon apparently never lost her admiration for Sitting Bull, contributing a laudatory piece on him to Thomas Bland's *A Brief History of the Late Military Invasion of the Home of the Sioux,* which was published in 1891. According to Pollack, the contribution appears to argue for her having been in communication, at least by letter, with members of Sitting Bull's family after his death.[25]

INTO THE SPIRIT WORLD

Not long after arriving at Standing Rock, Sitting Bull experienced a disturbing vision, one that, like other visions he had received, he took quite seriously. He went out alone early one morning to a location several miles away where he had hobbled some horses. There, he heard a voice speaking to him and discovered it to be coming from a meadowlark, a bird that he claimed had saved his life from a buffalo bull many years before. The meadowlark warned Sitting Bull that Lakotas would kill him.[26] Sitting Bull may have recalled that prophecy a few years later when a group of his own people arrived at his cabin early one morning to arrest him.

Sitting Bull's refusal to acquiesce completely to James McLaughlin's plans for the Lakotas laid the groundwork for his arrest and death. The Ghost Dance was a precipitating factor in that McLaughlin believed it was delaying the Lakotas' acceptance of the white man's world, and he blamed Sitting Bull for encouraging the dance as he tended to blame the Hunkpapa chief for all opposition to his authority. So McLaughlin recommended that the man he saw as the primary troublemaker and obstructionist be arrested and removed to a place where he could not interfere with McLaughlin and his nation's plans for the Lakotas.[27]

McLaughlin, however, was willing to bide his time until winter set in, driving the Indians away from the dance and into greater isolation within their own homes. McLaughlin wanted his Indian police to enact the arrest rather than the military, and Lieutenant Colonel Drum at Fort Yates agreed. Not so, however, General Miles, who decided to move ahead with the arrest through his own personal representative, none other than Sitting Bull's old friend and former employer, Buffalo Bill Cody.

Buffalo Bill arrived at Fort Yates on November 28, accompanied by two members of his Wild West Show, Pony Bob Haslam and Frank "White Beaver" Powell. Cody had been drinking heavily and was in no condition to carry out the arrest that day. Mary Collins noted in her autobiography that Cody was so drunk he could not even speak coherently. McLaughlin and Drum, according to Collins, concocted a stratagem to keep Cody from carrying out the arrest. They sent a messenger after Cody to say that Sitting Bull was coming in to the fort by another route, buying time until McLaughlin and Drum could get Cody's orders rescinded.[28]

Actually, it was the day after his arrival that Cody started toward Sitting Bull's home, and he apparently had sobered up well overnight. The messenger was McLaughlin's interpreter, Louis Primeau, who managed to divert Cody from his mission. McLaughlin contacted Interior Secretary Noble by telegram, and Noble took the matter to President Benjamin Harrison. The President countermanded Miles's order, and Cody departed. Even if Cody had met Sitting Bull, it is unlikely that violence would have ensued between the two friends. It is also highly unlikely that Sitting Bull would have accompanied Cody back to Fort Yates, undoubtedly instead managing to put Cody off in favor of some future meeting.

Although successful in removing Cody, McLaughlin still had to await permission from General Miles for the arrest. On December 10, that directive arrived, ordering Drum to carry it out. Both McLaughlin and Drum agreed that the military would play only a backup role, allowing the police—the *ceska masza,* or metal breasts (so named because of the badges they wore on their chests)—to confront Sitting Bull.[29] McLaughlin apparently thought that the arrest would be less confrontational if done by the tribal police, or perhaps McLaughlin would derive more credit or personal pleasure from arresting Sitting Bull through his agency police force. Even with the police, however, McLaughlin knew there was danger of violent resistance on the part of Sitting Bull's supporters. He promised a pension to the family of any policeman killed in the attempt, a promise that would go unfulfilled for almost 40 years.[30]

Bull Head was assigned to lead the arrest. Sitting Bull's nephew One Bull, a member of the tribal police, had been fired, ostensibly because he supported the Ghost Dance. As the arrest date approached, McLaughlin sent One Bull to haul freight far enough away to prevent his assisting his uncle. Several policemen, including Crazy Walking, a captain, sensing what was in the offing, quit rather than participate. Some stayed but faced the event with great fear, Shave Head, for example, correctly predicting to his family that he would die in the attempt.[31] Many of the police, including Bull Head, had fought alongside Sitting Bull in the past and faced their duty with sorrow.[32]

McLaughlin planned to arrest Sitting Bull on December 20 but moved up the date when he heard that Sitting Bull was considering leaving Grand River for Pine Ridge Agency to meet with the Ghost Dance leaders, who, fearing an attack by soldiers, had fled to a refuge in the highlands. Sitting Bull decided to write to McLaughlin, stating his people's right to pray as they wished and expressing his plan to visit the Ghost Dance leaders. He dictated the letter on the evening of December 11 to his son-in-law, Andrew Fox, who in halting English explained that Sitting Bull wished to go there "to know This Pray," in other words, to learn more about the dance.[33] Sitting Bull's openness about his fact-finding intentions, his request for permission to make the trip, and the implication that he had not yet completely subscribed to the theology of the dance should have eased McLaughlin's worries but instead inflamed them.

McLaughlin received the letter on December 12 and immediately set in motion the arrest. Louis Primeau that same day informed Bull Head of Sitting Bull's plans and cautioned him not to allow Sitting Bull to leave the reservation, allowing Bull Head the latitude to do what was necessary if Sitting Bull persisted in leaving.[34]

Bull Ghost, who had delivered Sitting Bull's letter, returned without the permission from McLaughlin for which Sitting Bull had hoped. On December 13, a Saturday, One Elk learned from his policeman brother, Iron Thunder, of the impending arrest and then informed his close friend Jumping Bull, Sitting Bull's adopted brother, of the plan. Jumping Bull returned to Sitting Bull's cabin and helped to establish a guard throughout the night. In charge of the bodyguards was Catch the Bear, a bitter enemy of Bull Head. Throughout the night, Sitting Bull and his guards reminisced about the old days, including the buffalo hunts; but in the morning, Sunday, December 14, Sitting Bull told his guards to leave and spent the day quietly in camp while others danced the Ghost Dance.[35]

That night, Sitting Bull slept in his cabin without bodyguards. Also in the cabin were one of his wives, Seen by the Nation; his son Crow Foot, now 14 years old; one of his small children; One Bull's wife, Red Whirlwind; and two old men who were guests. Other members of his family, including his other wife, slept in a nearby cabin of Sitting Bull's.

As Sitting Bull slept, the policemen met at Bull Head's cabin, south of the Grand River near Sitting Bull's birthplace. After offering a Christian prayer, they set out about 4:00 A.M. moving east toward Sitting Bull's cabin. They stopped at Gray Eagle's home, and Sitting Bull's brother-in-law joined the group. A force of 44, they reached their destination about 6:00 A.M. Captain Edmond Fechet was bringing troops to back up the policemen, but Bull Head knew that his men would make the arrest. He could not have failed to know how dangerous the enterprise was.

Sitting Bull awoke to pounding on the door, the rush of feet across his floor, and a flickering match quickly extinguished before another match successfully lit a candle. Sergeant Shave Head informed Sitting Bull of the arrest. The two old men were permitted to leave, and Seen by the

Nation rushed to the other cabin to retrieve Sitting Bull's clothes. Sitting Bull resisted the hands that tried hurriedly to help him dress, and as he was shoved to the door braced himself against the doorframe.

As Sitting Bull emerged through the door, Bull Head and Shave Head were beside him, Sergeant Red Tomahawk at his back. They did not get far before Hunkpapas surrounded the policemen. Catch the Bear confronted Bull Head and urged his fellow Hunkpapas to protect Sitting Bull. Jumping Bull, trying to prevent violence, urged his brother not to resist. Young Crow Foot, according to some accounts, then upbraided his father for not showing his accustomed courage, although Vestal claimed that none of the policemen that he interviewed heard any such statement from the boy.[36] Getting Sitting Bull away was delayed while policemen brought up his horse, the gift from Buffalo Bill.

Sitting Bull may have proclaimed his decision not to leave with the policemen[37]; for certain, many angry supporters of the chief were calling out that they would not let him be taken. Suddenly Catch the Bear raised his Winchester rifle and fired, hitting Bull Head. As the wounded policeman fell, he aimed and fired, hitting Sitting Bull in the chest. Red Tomahawk at the same moment fired into Sitting Bull's head. Although Red Tomahawk is usually credited with killing the Hunkpapa leader, either shot, according to the army surgeon who examined Sitting Bull, would have been fatal.[38]

As the firing continued, Shave Head was shot in the stomach, Bull Head was hit several more times, four more policemen were killed, and Private Middle suffered a serious foot wound. Among Sitting Bull's supporters, Catch the Bear was killed first, followed by five more, including the unarmed Jumping Bull and Jumping Bull's son, Chase Them Wounded. Three other supporters were wounded.

According to many written accounts, Sitting Bull's gray horse, which had been taught to perform tricks during its performing days with Cody's circus, responded to the shooting by sitting down, raising its hoof, and commencing its routine. As Utley points out, Vestal does not identify the source for this account, and the incident may be more fiction than fact.[39]

Policemen carried the wounded Bull Head, Shave Head, and Middle into Sitting Bull's cabin. There they discovered Crow Foot hiding. Lone Man hit Crow Foot in the forehead with his rifle butt, and then, along with other policemen, shot him. Of the wounded policemen, only Middle survived, after losing his foot. With the subsequent deaths of Shave Head and Bull Head, the death toll would rise to 14: Sitting Bull, seven of his followers, and six policemen.

One Bull returned in time to hear firing. Informed of what had happened, he rushed to Sitting Bull's cabin, where policemen ordered him to leave. For two hours, the policemen tried to hold off Sitting Bull's supporters, until finally Captain Fechet arrived with his cavalry.

Sitting Bull lay outside the cabin where he had fallen. Holy Medicine, who had made shirts for the Ghost Dance, but whose brother, Strong Arm, was among the dead policemen, picked up a neck yoke and smashed it against Sitting Bull's face.[40] A soldier stopped him from continuing the desecration.

Inside Sitting Bull's cabin hung Catherine Weldon's portrait of the chief. Another irate policeman knocked it off the wall and slashed the canvas with the barrel of his gun. A lieutenant named Matthew Steele intervened to save the painting and later purchased it from Sitting Bull's widows.

The date was December 15, 1890. Sitting Bull was dead. The greatest of the Lakota leaders, the man of whom James Walsh of the Canadian Mounted Police wrote, "History does not tell us that a greater Indian than Bull ever lived," had journeyed to the Spirit World.[41] The world that he left would never be the same again.

NOTES

1. Quoted in Robert M. Utley, *The Lance and the Shield: The Life and Times of Sitting Bull* (1993; New York: Ballantine Books, 1994), 269.

2. For Sitting Bull's trip to the Crows, see Utley, *The Lance and the Shield*, 266–67; and Stanley Vestal, *Sitting Bull: Champion of the Sioux*, 2nd ed. (1957; Norman: University of Oklahoma Press, 1989), 251–54.

3. Vestal, *Sitting Bull*, 254.

4. This discussion of pieces of legislation and the Lakotas' responses is especially indebted to Utley's *Lance and the Shield*, 268–80; and Utley's *The Last Days of the Sioux Nation*, 2nd ed. (New Haven, CT: Yale University Press, 2004), 40–59.

5. Red Cloud observed that Crook "never lied to us." For the quotation, see John G. Bourke, *On the Border with Crook* (New York: Charles Scribner's Sons, 1891), 486.

6. Vestal examines McLaughlin's machinations in *Sitting Bull*, 258–60.

7. Utley, *Last Days*, 55.

8. James Mooney, *The Ghost Dance* (North Dighton, MA: JG Press, 1996), 126–35, 154–55; Utley, *Last Days*, 64–72. The Mooney book is a reprint of Part 2 of the *Fourteenth Annual Report of the Bureau of Ethnology* and is based on Mooney's first-hand observations in the early 1890s.

9. Mooney, 151–53.

10. Mooney, 284–88.

11. Mooney, 274.

12. For an extensive discussion of Sitting Bull's attitudes toward religion, see Colin F. Taylor, *Sitting Bull and the White Man's Religion* (Wyk, Germany: Verlag für Amerikanistik D. Kuegler, 2000).

13. Utley, *The Lance and the Shield*, 287–89.

14. Mary Collins' autobiography, published in Stanley Vestal's *New Sources of Indian History: 1850–1891* (Norman: University of Oklahoma Press, 1934), 61–73.

15. See Collins, 61–73, for the information and quotations provided in this discussion.

16. Eileen Pollack, *Woman Walking Ahead: In Search of Catherine Weldon and Sitting Bull* (Albuquerque: University of New Mexico Press, 2002), 111.

17. Pollack, 89.

18. Pollack, especially 101–02, 107, 111–13; and Vestal, *Sitting Bull*, 263–70.

19. Pollack, 117, 121–27.

20. For a recent discussion of religious issues involving Mormons, Indians (including the Ghost Dance), and Euroamericans, see Todd M. Kerstetter, *God's Country, Uncle Sam's Land* (Champaign: University of Illinois Press, 2006).

21. Pollack, 136–42, 262–67.

22. Pollack, 321.

23. Pollack, 271. For the texts of the letters, see Vestal, *New Sources*, 103–10.

24. Pollack, 270–75.

25. Pollack, 281–82.

26. Utley, *The Lance and the Shield*, 290; Vestal, *Sitting Bull*, 20–21.

27. Much of this section, unless otherwise noted, is indebted to Utley's books.

28. Vestal, *New Sources*, 70–71. Also see Larry McMurtry, *The Colonel and Little Missie: Buffalo Bill, Annie Oakley, and the Beginnings of Superstardom in America* (New York: Simon and Schuster, 2005), 178–80; and Louis S. Warren, *Buffalo Bill's America: William Cody and the Wild West Show* (New York: Alfred A. Knopf, 2005), 379–80.

29. Utley *The Lance and the Shield*, 293–95.

30. Vestal, *Sitting Bull*, 313.

31. Vestal, *Sitting Bull*, 273–74.

32. Utley, *The Lance and the Shield*, 298.

33. Vestal, *Sitting Bull*, 283–85.

34. Utley, *The Lance and the Shield*, 296.

35. Vestal, *Sitting Bull*, 288–91.

36. Vestal, *Sitting Bull*, 298.

37. Vestal, *Sitting Bull*, 300.

38. Vestal, *Sitting Bull*, 304.

39. Utley, *The Lance and the Shield*, 396n.

40. Vestal, *Sitting Bull*, 305.

41. Quoted in Utley, *The Lance and the Shield*, 307.

Chapter 10

IN SEARCH OF SITTING BULL (1890–THE PRESENT)

SITTING BULL'S BURIAL

The body of Sitting Bull was loaded onto a wagon underneath the dead tribal policemen and transported to Fort Yates. Private J. F. Waggoner, a soldier assigned to the carpentry detail, constructed a wooden coffin six feet four inches long, two feet deep, and two feet wide. Waggoner recalled that a number of soldiers came into the shop where he was working and drove a nail each into the coffin, interpreting the gesture as an act of honor. Waggoner performed his duty with sorrow, remembering that Sitting Bull had eaten meals in his house and that he was, in Waggoner's words, "a fighter, a thinker, a chief, and a gentleman."[1]

On December 17, the coffin was taken to the Dead House (what passed for a morgue), and Sitting Bull, wrapped in a blanket, was placed in it. The lid was set loosely on the coffin, and Sitting Bull was transported to a corner of the Fort Yates military cemetery for burial. The lid was removed, chloride of lime poured over Sitting Bull, the lid nailed into place, and the coffin lowered into the grave. The quicklime was added to desiccate the body, a way of removing moisture that may also have helped preserve the body.

Sitting Bull was laid to rest among the soldiers who had once been his enemies. The placement might have seemed ironic to some, but placing one warrior among others probably would have appealed to Sitting Bull much more than being buried in the Catholic cemetery where the dead policemen were interred.

Most of Sitting Bull's family were temporarily held at Fort Yates, during which almost all of the dead chief's possessions were stolen. Sitting Bull's gray horse was bought back by Buffalo Bill from Sitting Bull's widows and returned to performing. It held an honored place in the Wild West Show, leading the procession and bearing the individual who carried the American flag. The cabin where Sitting Bull had spent his last night alive was also purchased from the widows, to be dismantled and then reconstructed in Chicago for the World's Fair of 1892. Agent McLaughlin, who had pushed for Sitting Bull's arrest and removal and, therefore to a great extent, was responsible for his death, kept a lock of his old adversary's hair. It later was found among McLaughlin's papers.[2]

Of the surviving family members, only One Bull remained at Grand River on the Standing Rock Reservation. The rest of the family moved south to Pine Ridge Reservation, wanting to get far away from the scene of their kinsman's death.

Sitting Bull's death produced a great deal of criticism in the press. Some newspapers labeled the death an assassination and "cold-blooded, premeditated murder."[3] In reality, McLaughlin apparently preferred to have Sitting Bull taken alive, and Bull Head tried to do that. The criticism did not prevent McLaughlin from having a long and successful career. He later became an Indian inspector for the Interior Department and died on the job in 1923 at the age of 74. Yet he never entirely escaped criticism over his role in Sitting Bull's death, and in his memoirs strongly defended his actions.[4]

When Fort Yates was dismantled in 1903, the bodies of the soldiers were moved, leaving Sitting Bull to lie alone. A wooden marker bore the words:

> Sitting Bull
> Died Dec. 15, 1890

The wooden marker proved a popular memento, and it had to be replaced regularly. Eventually, a stone cairn was erected at the foot of Sitting Bull's grave. Vestal was told that the grave was opened at that time, and Sitting Bull's skeleton seen still intact. Gradually, as increasing numbers of sightseers visited, improvements to the grave were made: an iron railing, a slab of cement, and a marble tombstone stating:

> Sitting Bull
> Died
> Dec. 15, 1890
> Chief of the
> Hunkpapa
> Sioux

Clarence Gray Eagle, son of Gray Eagle, Sitting Bull's brother-in-law who had joined the policemen to help arrest Sitting Bull, worked for years to have his remains moved from the military cemetery to a more appropriate site. As a child Clarence Gray Eagle had watched Sitting Bull die and perhaps felt, if not guilt over his father's role, at least a sense of duty to honor the great leader with a more fitting burial location.

After Clarence Gray Eagle's efforts repeatedly failed, he and several other men descended on the grave during a night in April 1953 and removed Sitting Bull's remains. They reburied him on a high point overlooking the Missouri River near the town of Mobridge, South Dakota. For the new burial site, near where Sitting Bull had been born, the sculptor Korczak Ziolkowski created a 12-foot-tall monument to the Hunkpapa leader.

Uncertainty persists as to which location actually contains Sitting Bull's remains. Assertions have continued since 1953 that the wrong bones were taken from the Fort Yates site, or that only some of the bones were removed. Whatever the case, efforts as of this writing are underway to improve both sites. The precise location of Sitting Bull's true burial place is far less important than the stature and accomplishments of the man when he was alive.

THE END OF THE GHOST DANCE

The death of Sitting Bull did not immediately end the Ghost Dance. Were it not for the continuing belief in the dance and the restoration that it promised, a violent response to Sitting Bull's death might have ensued. Instead, many Lakotas continued to believe that the new world was imminent, and if so, Sitting Bull would be among those who would return.

Despite the Ghost Dance, however, many Hankpapas feared additional violence by the government and fled to Pine Ridge Reservation to take refuge with Chief Red Cloud. Others hurried to the Miniconjou Big Foot, also known as Spotted Elk, who also started toward Pine Ridge. With Sitting Bull dead, Big Foot had moved to the top of the list of Lakota chiefs that the military wanted apprehended.[5]

On December 28, 1890, at Porcupine Creek in southwestern South Dakota, Big Foot, seriously ill with pneumonia, saw soldiers nearby. Major Samuel Whitside informed Big Foot that he had orders to escort the Miniconjou chief and his people to a military camp at Wounded Knee Creek, a few miles closer to the Nebraska line. When they arrived at Wounded Knee, a count showed 120 men and 230 women and children. Whitside decided to wait until morning to disarm Big Foot's party, and during the night Colonel James Forsyth arrived with additional troops. As Big Foot slept fitfully, struggling to breathe with his illness, four Hotchkiss guns, each capable of firing nearly 50 two-pound shells per minute, were trained on the sleeping Indians.

The next morning, confiscation of weapons began after breakfast. Unsatisfied with the number of guns turned over to the soldiers, Forsyth sent troopers into the tents to search for more weapons. Then the Indians were ordered to remove the blankets they were wearing in case they were concealing weapons underneath. The soldiers were unaware that Big Foot and his band were wearing Ghost Shirts, which they believed would protect them from the soldiers' bullets. When Black Coyote raised his rifle over his head and declared that he would not turn over his gun, soldiers grabbed him and spun him around. Somehow a gun went off.

That single shot instantly precipitated massive firing and chaos. The Hotchkiss guns rained death down on the Miniconjous. When the fighting was over, Big Foot and more than 150 Indians lay dead or mortally wounded, many of them women and children. Some estimates put the death figure as high as 300. In all, 25 soldiers were dead and 39 wounded, many from friendly fire as they grappled in close combat with the Indians.

At Wounded Knee, not far from where Crazy Horse's parents in 1877 had buried their dead son's heart and bones, Sioux resistance, for all practical purposes, died with Big Foot.[6] Minor skirmishes occurred into the new year, but any serious opposition was over. The Ghost Shirts had proven to be only cloth after all. Crazy Horse, Sitting Bull, and now Big Foot were dead. The promise of the Ghost Dance was an illusion. The old way of life was over, and it would not return. Many had tried to keep the past alive, none more successfully than Sitting Bull. Yet even he had ultimately been defeated by the overwhelming power of a new order.

REDISCOVERING SITTING BULL

Sitting Bull was a world-famous figure when he died in 1890, yet those who read about him, faced him in battle, plotted his defeat, or observed him as a member of Buffalo Bill's Wild West Show knew little about who he really was. As the years passed, and individuals who had known Sitting Bull died, much that he had accomplished was in danger of being lost to memory.

Fortunately, two individuals have done an extraordinary job of ensuring that Sitting Bull's place in history will endure. One of them, Walter Stanley Campbell, who wrote as Stanley Vestal, embarked on his biography of Sitting Bull at a time when many people who could offer first-hand accounts of the Hunkpapa leader were still alive, including Sitting Bull's nephews One Bull and White Bull.

Vestal's biography, *Sitting Bull: Champion of the Sioux*, was first published in 1932 and reissued in a revised edition in 1957. Vestal's biography has been criticized as overly romantic, almost hagiographic in approach. A major deficiency is the almost total lack of documentation, a great disappointment to anyone wishing to know where Vestal discovered specific information.

Nonetheless, Vestal engaged in extensive interviews with eyewitnesses and tells the story of Sitting Bull in a clear, chronological, and dramatic fashion, if somewhat too poetically at times. He also plays an invaluable role by placing Sitting Bull within the cultural context of his times. Vestal's effort, in the Sitting Bull biography as well as in other works mentioned in this volume, must engender respect and appreciation on the part of anyone trying to learn more about Sitting Bull. I readily acknowledge here, as well as in notes throughout this book, my indebtedness to Vestal and to the other giant figure in biographical writing about Sitting Bull, Robert M. Utley.

Utley's *The Lance and the Shield*, published in 1993, is in some respects a more scholarly work than its predecessor. No eyewitnesses remained alive when Utley began his biography, but he brought to his effort other scholarly approaches, including elements at least partly lacking in Vestal's book: clear and extensive documentation, an appreciative but more objective perspective on Sitting Bull than one receives from Vestal, and a measured tone that invites confidence in his research and conclusions.

All other books about Sitting Bull must pay homage to the work of Vestal and Utley. They have reclaimed Sitting Bull from both willful neglect and the natural erosion of memory. They have positioned him within history and created a convincing portrait of a man who was truly great—great in the eye of a romantic, great in the judgment of a historian.

Other biographers and historians have also helped modern students of history understand Sitting Bull's importance. These books range widely in scope. They include such disparate works as Albert Marrin's *Sitting Bull and His World*, written for younger readers; Grant MacEwan's *Sitting Bull: The Years in Canada*, an exploration of one significant period in its subject's life; and Gary C. Anderson's recent *Sitting Bull and the Paradox of Lakota Nationhood*, designed for use in college courses. Some authors, such as Dee Brown in *Bury My Heart At Wounded Knee*, have placed Sitting Bull within the larger context of the history of the American Indian.

A great number of other books have explored the Plains Indian war or, specifically, the Battle of Little Bighorn. Many such works are included in the bibliography that follows this chapter.

Perhaps one of the most important attempts to expand people's knowledge of Sitting Bull and honor him at the same time is the college named after him on Standing Rock Reservation: Sitting Bull College. The college has adopted as its motto a saying of Sitting Bull's: "Let us put our minds together to see what we can build for our children." There, on the reservation where Sitting Bull spent the last years of his life, more than the historical memory of Sitting Bull remains. Through this college, he continues still to do what he attempted so long and so hard during his life: to contribute toward a better life for his people.[7]

NOTES

1. For information on Sitting Bull's burial and the aftermath, I am especially indebted to Stanley Vestal, *Sitting Bull: Champion of the Sioux*, 2nd ed. (1957; Norman: University of Oklahoma Press, 1989), 308–15.

2. Vestal, 312.

3. Vestal, 310–11.

4. James McLaughlin, *My Friend the Indian* (Boston: Houghton Mifflin, 1910).

5. For accounts of what transpired at Wounded Knee, see Dee Brown, *Bury My Heart at Wounded Knee* (1971; New York: Bantam Books, 1972), 413–18; Robert M. Utley, *The Last Days of the Sioux Nation*, 2nd ed. (New Haven, CT: Yale University Press, 2004), 167–230; and James H. McGregor, *The Wounded Knee Massacre: From the Viewpoint of the Sioux*, 3rd ed. (Baltimore: Wirth Brothers, 1940).

6. For accounts of the burial of Crazy Horse, see Brown, 295–96; and Larry McMurtry, *Crazy Horse* (New York: Lipper/Viking, 1999), 140.

7. To learn about Sitting Bull College, visit <http://www.sittingbull.edu/>.

BIBLIOGRAPHY

PRINT SOURCES

Adams, Alexander B. *Sitting Bull: An Epic of the Plains*. New York: G. P. Putnam's Sons, 1973.

Anderson, Gary C. *Sitting Bull and the Paradox of Lakota Nationhood*. New York: Pearson Longman, 2007.

Baird, George W. "General Miles's Indian Campaigns." *Century Magazine* 42 (Jul. 1891): 351–70.

Bourke, John G. *On the Border with Crook*. New York: Charles Scribner's Sons, 1891.

Branch, E. Douglas. *The Hunting of the Buffalo*. Lincoln: University of Nebraska Press, 1929.

Brininstool, E. A. *Troopers with Custer: Historic Incidents of the Battle of the Little Bighorn*. 1952. Lincoln: University of Nebraska Press, 1989.

Brown, Dee. *The American West*. 1994. New York: Simon and Schuster, 1995.

———. *The Year of the Century: 1876*. New York: Charles Scribner's Sons, 1966.

———. *Bury My Heart at Wounded Knee: An Indian History of the American West*. 1971. New York: Bantam Books, 1972.

Bruno, Giberti. *Designing the Centennial: A History of the 1876 International Exhibition in Philadelphia*. Lexington: University Press of Kentucky, 2002.

Campbell, Lyle. *American Indian Languages: The Historical Linguistics of Native America*. New York: Oxford University Press, 1997.

Carroll, John M., ed. *Private Theodore Ewert's Diary of the Black Hills Expedition of 1874*. Piscataway, NJ: Consultant Resources Incorporated, 1976.

Carter, Robert A. *Buffalo Bill Cody: The Man Behind the Legend*. New York: John Wiley and Sons, 2000.

Chittenden, Hiram M., and Alfred T. Richardson, eds. *Life, Letters, and Travels of Father Pierre-Jean De Smet, S. J., 1801–1873*. 4 vols. New York: Francis P. Harper, 1905.

Clodfelter, Michael. *The Dakota War: The United States Army versus the Sioux, 1862–1865*. Jefferson, NC: McFarland, 1998.

Coel, Margaret. *The Story Teller*. 1998. New York: Penguin, 1999.

Cox, Hank H. *Lincoln and the Sioux Uprising of 1862*. Nashville: Cumberland House, 2005.

Cronau, Rudolf. "My Visit among the Hostile Dakota Indians and How They Became My Friends." *South Dakota Historical Collections* 22 (1946): 410–25.

Crook, George. *General George Crook: His Autobiography*. Ed. Martin F. Schmitt. Norman: University of Oklahoma Press, 1946.

Dahlstrom, Neil. *The John Deere Story: A Biography of Plowmakers John & Charles Deere*. DeKalb: Northern Illinois University Press, 2005.

DeBarthe, Joe. *Life and Adventures of Frank Grouard*, ed. Edgar I. Stewart. Norman: University of Oklahoma Press, 1958.

Denig, Edwin Thompson. *The Assiniboine*, ed. J.N.B. Hewitt. Regina: Canadian Plains Research Center, 2000.

Densmore, Frances. *Teton Sioux Music*. Bulletin 61. Washington, DC: Government Printing Office, 1918.

Derounian-Stodola, Kathryn Zabelle, ed. *Women's Indian Captivity Narratives*. New York: Penguin Books, 1998.

Ellis, Richard J. *To the Flag: The Unlikely History of the Pledge of Allegiance*. Lawrence: University of Kansas Press, 2005.

Ens, Gerhard J. *Homeland to Hinterland: The Changing Worlds of the Red River Métis in the Nineteenth Century*. Toronto: University of Toronto Press, 1996.

Evans, Sarah A. Written Statement. n.d. McCracken Research Library of the Buffalo Bill Historical Center, Cody, WY.

Ewers, John C. "When Sitting Bull Surrendered His Winchester." *Indian Life on the Upper Missouri*. Norman: University of Oklahoma Press, 1968. 175–81.

Fees, Paul. Letter to Robert M. Utley. 28 April 1992. McCracken Research Library of the Buffalo Bill Historical Center, Cody, WY.

Foley, Thomas W. *Father Francis M. Craft: Missionary to the Sioux*. Lincoln: University of Nebraska Press, 2002.

Gardner, Mark L. *Little Bighorn Battlefield National Monument*. Tucson: Western National Parks Association, 2005.

Garraghan, Gilbert J., S. J. "Father De Smet's Sioux Peace Mission of 1868 and the Journal of Charles Galpin." *Mid-America* 13 (1930): 141–63.

Gates, Paul Wallace. *Free Homesteads for All Americans: The Homestead Act of 1862*. Washington, DC: Civil War Centennial Commission, 1962.

Gibbon, Guy. *The Sioux: The Dakota and Lakota Nations*. Malden, MA: Blackwell, 2003.

Godfrey, E. S. Letter to E. S. Paxson. 16 Jan. 1896. McCracken Research Library of the Buffalo Bill Historical Center, Cody, WY.

Grafe, Ernest and Paul Horsted. *Exploring with Custer: The 1874 Black Hills Expedition*. 3rd ed. Custer, SD: Golden Valley Press, 2005.

Gray, John S. *Centennial Campaign: The Sioux War of 1876*. Ft. Collins, CO: The Old Army Press, 1976.

Greene, Jerome A., ed. Lakota and Cheyenne: *Indian Views of the Great Sioux War, 1878–1877*. Norman: University of Oklahoma Press, 1994.

———. *Slim Buttes: An Episode of the Great Sioux War*. Norman: University of Oklahoma Press, 1982.

———. Yellowstone Command: *Colonel Nelson A. Miles and the Great Sioux War, 1878–1877*. 1991. Norman: University of Oklahoma Press, 2006.

Haines, Francis. *The Buffalo*. New York: Thomas Y. Crowell, 1970.

Hassrick, Royal B. *The Sioux: Life and Customs of a Warrior Society*. Norman: University of Oklahoma Press, 1964.

Havighurst, Walter. *Annie Oakley of the Wild West*. New York: Macmillan, 1954.

Haydon, A. L. *The Riders of the Plains: A Record of the Royal North-West Mounted Police of Canada, 1873–1910*. Toronto: Copp Clark Company, 1910.

Jackson, Donald Dean. *Custer's Gold: The United States Cavalry Expedition of 1874*. 1966. Lincoln: University of Nebraska Press, 1972.

———, ed. *Letters of the Lewis and Clark Expedition with Related Documents 1783–1854*. Urbana: University of Illinois Press, 1962.

Kappler, Charles J., ed. *Indian Affairs: Laws and Treaties*. 7 vols. 1904–41. Washington, DC: U.S. Government Printing Office, 1975–79.

Kelly, Fanny. *Narrative of my Captivity among the Sioux Indians*. Cincinnati: Wilstach, Baldwin & Co., 1871.

———. *Narrative of My Captivity among the Sioux Indians*, ed. Clark and Mary Lee Spence. Old Saybrook, CT: Konecky and Konecky, 1990.

Kerstetter, Todd M. *God's Country, Uncle Sam's Land*. Champaign: University of Illinois Press, 2006.

Killoren, John J. *"Come, Blackrobe": De Smet and the Indian Tragedy*. Norman: University of Oklahoma Press, 1994.

Larson, Robert W. "Gall: 'The Fighting Cock of the Sioux.'" *Wild West* June 2006: 26–32.

———. "Lakota Chief Red Cloud: Formidable in War and Peace." *Chiefs and Generals: Nine Men Who Shaped the American West*, ed. Richard W. Etulain and Glenda Riley. Golden, CO: Fulcrum Publishing, 2004. 1–18.

———. Red Cloud: *Warrior-Statesman of the Lakota Sioux*. Norman: University of Oklahoma Press, 1997.

Lemann, Nicholas. *Redemption: The Last Battle of the Old Civil War*. New York: Farrar, Straus and Giroux, 2006.

Lubetkin, M. John. *Jay Cook's Gamble: The Northern Pacific Railroad, the Sioux and the Panic of 1873*. Norman: University of Oklahoma Press, 2006.

Luther Standing Bear. *My Indian Boyhood*. 1931. Lincoln: University of Nebraska Press, 1988.

———. *My People the Sioux*. 1928. Lincoln: University of Nebraska Press, 1975.

MacEwan, Grant. *Sitting Bull: The Years in Canada*. Edmonton: Hurtig Publishers, 1973.

Marrin, Albert. *Sitting Bull and His World*. New York: Dutton Children's Books, 2000.

McCabe, James D. *The Illustrated History of the Centennial Exhibition*. Philadelphia: National Publishing Company, 1876.

McCormick, Cyrus. *The Century of the Reaper: An Account of Cyrus Hall McCormick, the Inventor of the Reaper*. Boston: Houghton Mifflin, 1931.

McGregor, James H. *The Wounded Knee Massacre: From the Viewpoint of the Sioux*. 3rd ed. Baltimore: Wirth Brothers, 1940.

McHugh, Tom. *The Time of the Buffalo*. New York: Alfred A. Knopf, 1972.

McLaughlin, James. *My Friend the Indian*. Boston: Houghton Mifflin, 1910.

McMurtry, Larry. *The Colonel and Little Missie: Buffalo Bill, Annie Oakley, and the Beginnings of Superstardom in America*. New York: Simon and Schuster, 2005.

———. *Oh What a Slaughter: Massacres in the American West*. New York: Simon and Schuster, 2005.

Michno, Gregory F. *Lakota Noon: The Indian Narrative of Custer's Defeat*. 1997. Missoula, MT: Mountain Press Publishing Company, 2004.

Michno, Susan J. "The Spirit Lake Massacre: Death and Captivity." *Wild West* (Feb. 2006): 46–52.

Miles, Nelson A. *Personal Recollections and Observations of General Nelson A. Miles*. Chicago: Werner, 1896.

Miller, David Humphreys. *Custer's Fall: The Native American Side of the Story*. 1957. New York: Meridian, 1992.

Mooney, James. *The Ghost Dance*. North Dighton, MA: JG Press, 1996.

Nerburn, Kent. *Chief Joseph and the Flight of the Nez Perce*. New York: HarperSanFrancisco, 2005.

Pfaller, Louis. "Enemies in '76, Friends in '85-Sitting Bull and Buffalo Bill." *Prologue, the Journal of the National Archives* 1.2 (1969): 16–31.

Pollack, Eileen. *Woman Walking Ahead: In Search of Catherine Weldon and Sitting Bull*. Albuquerque: University of New Mexico Press, 2002.

Ostler, Jeffrey. *The Plains Sioux and U.S. Colonialism from Lewis and Clark to Wounded Knee*. New York: Cambridge University Press, 2004.

Robinson, Charles M. III. *The Plains War 1757–1900*. Osceola, WI: Osprey, 2003.

Roe, Frank Gilbert. *The Indian and the Horse*. Norman: University of Oklahoma Press, 1962.

Sitting Bull. *A New Pictographic Autobiography of Sitting Bull*, ed. Alexis Praus. Washington, DC: Smithsonian Institution, 1955.

———. *Three Pictographic Autobiographies of Sitting Bull*, ed. M. W. Stirling. Washington, DC: Smithsonian Institution, 1938.

Sprague, Donovan Arleigh. *Standing Rock Sioux. Images of America Series.* Chicago: Arcadia Publishing, 2004.

Sundstrom, Linea. "The Sacred Black Hills: An Ethnohistorical Review." *Great Plains Quarterly* 17 [Summer/Fall] (1997): 185–212.

Swartout, Annie Fern. *Missie, An Historical Biography of Annie Oakley*. Blanchester, OH: Brown Publishing Company, 1947

Tankersley, Kenneth B., and Robert B. Pickering. *Sitting Bull's Pipe: Rediscovering the Man, Correcting the Myth*. Wyk, Germany: Tataka Press, 2006.

Taylor, Colin F. *Sitting Bull and the White Man's Religion*. Wyk, Germany: Verlag für Amerikanistik D. Kuegler, 2000.

Turney-High, Harry Holbert. *The Flathead Indians of Montana*. Menasha, WI: American Anthropological Association, 1937.

Utley, Robert M. *The Indian Frontier of the American West, 1846–1890*. Albuquerque: University of New Mexico Press, 1984.

———. *The Lance and the Shield: The Life and Times of Sitting Bull*. 1993. New York: Ballantine Books, 1994.

———. *The Last Days of the Sioux Nation*. 2nd ed. New Haven, CT: Yale University Press, 2004.

Vestal, Stanley. *New Sources of Indian History 1850–1891*. Norman: University of Oklahoma Press, 1934.

———. *Sitting Bull: Champion of the Sioux*. 2nd ed. 1957. Norman: University of Oklahoma Press, 1989.

———. *Warpath: The True Story of the Fighting Sioux Told in a Biography of Chief White Bull*. 1934. Lincoln: University of Nebraska Press, 1984.

Wakefield, Sarah F. *Six Weeks in the Sioux Tepees*. 1863. Guilford, CT: Globe Pequot, 2004.

Walker, James R. *Lakota Belief and Ritual*, ed. Raymond J. DeMallie and Elaine A. Jahner. 1980. Lincoln: University of Nebraska Press, 1991.

Warren, Louis S. *Buffalo Bill's America: William Cody and the Wild West Show*. New York: Alfred A. Knopf, 2005.

White Bull. *Lakota Warrior*, ed. and trans. James H. Howard. 1968. Lincoln: University of Nebraska Press, 1996.

Wooden Leg. *Wooden Leg: A Warrior Who Fought Custer.* Interpreted by Thomas B. Marquis. 1957. Lincoln: University of Nebraska Press, 1962.

Wooster, Robert. *Nelson A. Miles and the Twilight of the Frontier Army.* 1995. Lincoln: University of Nebraska Press, 1996.

Yenne, Bill. *The Encyclopedia of North American Indian Tribes: A Comprehensive Study of Tribes from the Abitibi to the Zuni.* North Dighton, MA: JG Press, 1989.

ELECTRONIC SOURCES

Buffalo Bill Historical Center <http://www.bbhc.org/home/index.cfm> (information abut the Plains Indians, William F. Cody, and other aspects of Western life).

Chief Sitting Bull <http://www.sittingbull.org/> (section of the Museum of History site devoted to Sitting Bull).

Lakota Language Consortium <http://www.lakhota.org/> (educational resources related to efforts to keep the Lakota language alive).

Sitting Bull College <http://www.sittingbull.edu/> (site for the college on Standing Rock Reservation named in honor of Sitting Bull).

Standing Rock Sioux Tribe <http://www.standingrock.org/> (information about the history of the Sioux and the reservation).

INDEX

About the Author

EDWARD J. RIELLY, Professor of English at St. Joseph's College in Maine, has taught on Western film and the history of the West for many years. He is the author of several nonfiction books including *F. Scott Fitzgerald: A Biography* (Greenwood, 2005), and *The 1960s* (Greenwood, 2003). He has also published 10 books of poetry.